PRICELESS
The Making of a Rare Jewel

Frenise L. Mann

Published by 4-P Publishing
Chattanooga, TN

Book Cover Design: MS Design & Photography – Chattanooga, TN

Printed in the United States
ISBN-13: 978-1941749036

To order this book or request the author to be a guest speaker at your event, please visit www.TheMentorFM.com or email TheMentorFM@gmail.com.

DEDICATION

I dedicate this book, to my younger sister, Jarita McClendon. I pray
that you will know that God has made you a rare jewel for His
Kingdom.
I dedicate this book to every young lady who God has brought into
my life to mentor, past, present and future.

This is my testimony.

ACKNOWLEDGMENTS

I want to first thank my Heavenly Father, for choosing me to be His daughter, for giving me the strength to rise up and live an abundant life in spite of disappointments, world circumstances and trials. I want to thank my husband, Carlos Mann, who is truly the "Mann" of my life. I appreciate his patience and sacrifice of missing date nights together so that I could write this book. My husband is truly an example of the faith that God desires His people to walk and live by. I love you dearly!

I want to thank Laura Brown and the S.W.A.T. crew for stretching me, your encouragement and pulling me out of my comfort zone. I want to thank my Pastors and friends, Dr. David and Sylvia Banks. Thanks for being on my cheerleader team, for all the gifts, encouragement and believing in me. I am privileged to know you and inspired by your lifestyle to be kings of the earth.

I want to thank my family. My mother Wynona McClendon, a strong and beautiful woman, who has encouraged me, supported me, cried with me, and loved me through it all. You are still the woman I look up too. My dad, Frederick McClendon, II, who has loved me in his own special way. To my siblings, Vivian Johnson, Fred McClendon, III, Jarita McClendon and Nicolas Abbott, for all the laughter and tears; we are still here and the best is yet to come.

To my God-parents
Gary and Rosalyn Hickman and LeMont and Renita Johnson.
Gary and Rosalyn, you make me smile. Thanks for feeding me, loving me, and encouraging me to shine bright! Momma Rosalyn thank you for your prayers, Godly insight and hope.
LeMont and Renita Johnson, you are rock solid. Thanks for feeding me, the gifts, and the laughter. Momma Renita, thank you for the quiet talks, hope and wisdom.
To both my God Fathers, Chef Lemont and Paw-Paw Gary. I am glad that God brought you into my life, to show me how to receive the love of an earthly father, unconditionally and without performance. You hold a special place in my heart, forever.

And last, but not least, my cheerleader crew, Aqua, Alexis, DeSharla, Vanessa Cavelle, the girls at work: Christina, Lou, and Samantha. To my editors, Sylvia Banks and Mariann Martin, the ladies of book focus group, and book cover designer Mike Simmons. Thank you, tremendously! We did it! It is finished.

Table of Contents

PREFACE

As a little girl, I always dreamed of being married, having a husband, two children (a boy and a girl, the boy being the oldest of course) a huge house with a circular driveway and working as a secretary for a major company. Also, my name would be, Linda Carter, like <u>Wonder Woman</u> on the *Super Friends*. I believe that every little girl has dreams like these of some sort, where you always play house and work at some company or stay home with the children and bake cookies. However, I soon discovered that this was not the reality of the world that I would grow up in. In order for me to obtain the dream that I thought was my reality, I would have to walk through life's journey of self-discovery. Self-discovery – is the act or process of achieving understanding or knowledge of oneself. (Farlex, 2014)

Being single in the 21st century is definitely a journey of self-discovery. From *Being Mary Jane* to eHarmony internet dating, the single woman of today is definitely trying to find out who she is and where she belongs. Even though she possess what I call the Four-S', saved, smart, savvy, and sexy, single women of today are still looking for love in all the wrong places. Well, this is the book that will unfold the mysteries of who you truly are, why you exist and lead you on the path of being single, with joy, peace, love and a successful life.

Anything of true value takes effort, time and patience to find. Like gold, copper or rare jewels. Jewels are known as precious, valuable stones that have been cut and shaped. There are several types of jewels from rubies and sapphires to pearls and onyx. However, rare jewels are created deep down in the earth's crust and the Master's hand is the one that brings it to the surface. One well known rare jewel is a diamond. Diamonds are formed in pitch-dark, deep down in the mantle of the earth's crust from carbon and volcanic activity. Proverbs 3:15 NASB says "She is more precious than jewels: And nothing you desire compares with her." Everything that God has created, He said, is good. So my queen, you are that diamond, you are that precious jewel. Muhammad Ali once asked his daughter some thought provoking questions. "Where do you find diamonds? Deep down in the ground, covered and protected. Where do you find pearls? Deep down at the bottom of the ocean, covered up and protected in a beautiful shell. Where do you find gold? Way down in the mine, covered over with layers and layers of rock." If you are reading this book, then perhaps you have been through hell and then some, but know it was only God's formation of bringing a rare jewel into the earth realm.

Albert Einstein said, "Doing the same thing over and over again and expecting different results is insanity." So, are you ready to make a decision to do something different? Are you tired of being tired, of being tired of the same old relationships? Do you find yourself doing things for a man that you promised yourself that you would never do? Then you have picked up the right book at the right time. This is the book that will challenge you and stretch you to rise up and embrace your journey of becoming a rare jewel, knowing that you will come forth as a true diamond. Allow the God of all creation to shape you, cut you, and form you into that lustrous stone that will be placed into a crown that God has predestined for you, my queen. Take a bow my queen, you do deserve a King!

I pray that this book will empower you to be different, intentionally, to feel accepted in your own skin and to know without a shadow of doubt that you were created on purpose and to fulfill your own destiny. You were designed to leave an indelible mark.

INTRODUCTION

"We must pay a price if we are to become priceless."

— Elizabeth George

Girlfriends getting together to surprise one of their friends for her 30th birthday.
Blind fold, tank of gas and coffee: $120
Full Spa Day at Spa Sydell in Atlanta, GA: $150
Dinner at Houston's: $50
Tickets to see A Christmas Carol: $65
Meeting and taking a picture with Tyler Perry - Very Surprising!!
Making memorable moments with my friends full of love, joy and laughter all day - Priceless!

Some of you may remember the, "Priceless MasterCard", commercials which depicted people spending money on material things like football tickets, dinners, or plane tickets. The above example was a personal surprise birthday card, I created for a girlfriend, mimicking the Priceless commercials. The ultimate experience of spending quality time with family or friends is the greatest value; which is priceless.

What does the world really hold valuable in the 21st century? Better yet, what does the woman of the 21st century hold valuable? As I made a decision to write this book and began my research, I found out that many women of the 21st century take their value or worth from images of reality shows, celebrities or men. One television show that is very popular today amongst young African-American women is, *Being Mary Jane*. As I watched another episode, for my research, of course, I saw that the main character, Mary Jane, who is played by the popular Gabrielle Union had won an Image Award. I was appalled at the fact, the award was given for her character portrayal of being Mary Jane!! When I looked up the definition of image it read, "The physical likeness or representation of a person, animal or thing." (Farlex, 2014) When I think that *Being Mary Jane* won an image award that represent the image of all women, especially African-American females in today's society, it grieves me to think that people, especially females, will really portray women as the image that this TV series portrays.

Let's see, Mary Jane is a single African-American female, who is attractive, talented, educated and successful. She prides herself on being a hard worker, physically in shape and in touch with family and friends. She has a beautiful house, drives a Porsche and like most women of today, she has problems with men. For instance she had an affair with a married man. When she discovered that he was married she found herself entangled in a web that she could not get out of. Along with the affair, she still "loves" this other man that she shot to the curb. She wants him back, however he has a new woman in his life and she is Caucasian, which adds more drama to the story. I thought to myself, Wow! what an image for women of today. A television show that engraves an image upon the brains of my sisters that this is all you are worth. Women were not designed to be sexually active before marriage. This circumstance has taken us so far away from our original design, that it takes true brokenness and humility to emerge before we will be able to receive our true identity and worth in Christ Jesus. Priceless: The Making of a Rare Jewel is just the book that every struggling woman needs to read.

So the question remains, what is the true value or worth of a woman? One day, as I am getting ready for work, I received a text early in the morning, from a young lady. She informed me for the umpteenth time that her boyfriend just texted her and that he does not see himself marrying her because it just seems weird and yet with the same breath he declares that he loves her. This text came on one of the most important days of her life. She was getting ready to interview for a prominent position. And he called to break up with her again. Now, this is just nonsense! If a man tells you that he loves you, but does not want to marry you over and over again, then you may need to adhere to the words that are coming out of his mouth. It is sad to recognize that most women ignore these signs. You may ask, why do we ignore the signs or the red flags? Because we find ourselves being desperate, vulnerable, and having low self-esteem. We do not know our true identity, who we really are, why we exist and what is our purpose in life. If it is not to be a man's wife, then what is it? So, we try to change the man whether we do it consciously or unconsciously. We wait on him. In the process we get abused, misused, and confused. With our educated selves, we waste days, months and years in debilitating relationships, only to be left alone again calculating all the time we invested. No woman should endure this foolishness again and again. Ladies, we must first learn to love ourselves, so that we will know what true love really is. "Love does not hold a list of wrong doings, it does not provoke, it believes all things, hopes all things, love never fails." I Corinthians 13. In order to get different results, one must try something different. Let the man go, until he realizes how valuable you truly are. A woman was designed to be loved like Christ loved the church, not like a puppy that a person feels like being bothered with today and then tomorrow they don't. You are worth more than that. A true woman of God must know her original design by God and how He views her.

Society has made it acceptable for open relationships, orgies, girls kissing each other publically, lesbians, same sex marriages, ride or die chicks, sex with multiple partners at the same time and oral sex as the norm or technical virginity and who knows what else. However, where does this leave the woman of today; lonely, estranged, broken, disappointed, in despair, hopeless, and confused. We are comfortable being the "main woman" knowing that there are other women our man has on the side or we become the "second woman." We are overwhelmed and in survival mode, numb or just existing.

Hence, the reason for this book. <u>Priceless: The Making of a Rare Jewel</u> holds the answer to the struggles or problems that women face today.

I have discovered that people in general put value into luxury homes, expensive cars, and social status. Some people find value in collecting things such as stamps, antiques, art and precious stones. I found out, that out of all of these things, precious stones are the most unique items that can be truly valuable. Precious stones have various names, such as gem stones, gems or jewels. They can also be called by the actual type of stone they become, pearls, rubies, amethysts, or emeralds. Many times we hear that diamonds are a girl's best friend. Well, this does have some ironic concepts and principles that single women of today, can glean from when it comes to the making or the formation of a diamond and living a victorious life as a single woman.

The making of a diamond can be fascinating, especially when you think about how and where diamonds come from. The word diamond is derived from the Greek meaning "unbreakable". This name is very fitting when I think about the process of becoming a rare jewel. Diamonds are created from a carbon substance that forms into a crystal structure called a diamond lattice. Because of the extremely hard lattice only few impurities can contaminate a diamond. Most natural diamonds are formed at high temperature and pressure at depths of 140 to 190 kilometers (87 to 118 mi) in the

Earth's mantle. (Diamond, n.d.) Diamonds are brought close to the Earth's surface only through deep volcanic eruptions by a magma, which is smolten hot rock. Diamonds are the hardest substance known to man. It spreads light very well and appears in different colors. There are natural made diamonds, and there are also, synthetic diamonds, which are man made. The natural diamonds are the most valuable and can not be duplicated.

When I think about the creation of a natural diamond and the life of the 21st century single woman there are many similarities. The single woman comes in all shapes, sizes and colors, just like a diamond. A natural diamond is only found deep within the Earth. It has to be cut, taken through extreme pressure and heat, before it can spread the brillant light and luster it was designed to shine forth. As the carbon substance breaks through the cooling stages, one can begin to see the intricate curves and edges of a priceless diamond. The same is also true of a valuable single woman. She may find herself deep down in the Earth's dark places. She may even have to go through several pressures, such as an identity crisis, low self-esteem and past disappointments. As life's heated circumstances of wrong relationships, mental and physical abuse, and having no father tries to deplete the single woman of today, she can still emerge victoriously. The only answer to becoming a diamond of priceless value is knowing and accepting who designed and created the woman. It is God, who is Abba, which means Father.

I pray as you read this book, that you are transformed from the inside out and the light of the Father shines forth and through all the pain, despair, and struggles you may have faced. You were born to be a diamond. So let's take this journey together and let me show you that you are valuable. You are worthy. You are priceless!

As you read this book, you will notice at the end of each chapter there are Prayers and Empowerment Confessions for you to meditate on for your own healing, deliverance and wholeness. I pray that you will dwell on these truths and allow them to take root in your heart, mind and soul.

* The names used in the book have been changed to protect the identity of the individuals mentioned.*

PART ONE: THE PITCH-DARK
THE PAST IS "JUST THAT" THE PAST

"A fine glass vase goes from treasure to trash, the moment it is broken. Fortunately, something else happens to you and me. Pick up your pieces. Then, help me gather mine."
— Vera Nazarian, The Perpetual Calendar of Inspiration

Everyone that is born wants to believe that they are of true value. However, the cares of the world begins to dictate to them a different belief. I remember as a little girl, I thought the world was a beautiful place. I loved to be outside, barefoot, laying in the grass, looking up at the sky, making animal and objects out of the clouds that went by. I loved to look at the colorful hot air balloons and wondered how they were going to land and where they would land. I grew up living on top of a hill in a cul-de-sac. In this circle, I would dance in the rain with an umbrella, bare foot and sing the song, "Singing in the Rain."

What a life to enjoy. As I grew older, I realized there were people in the world that did not share my same view of the world. I had to be in the sixth grade, probably about 11 years old, when my world of song and dance quickly began to change. My mother worked second shift, so my siblings and I were left at home alone a lot. I remember going next door to Mr. and Mrs. Thomas' house to borrow a cup of sugar to make some Kool-Aid. Something that I had done several times before for my mom, but this time would prove to be different. It was getting dark outside and I put on my pink robe and house shoes. I remember that it was one of those robes that you stepped into and it zipped up the front. I grabbed a big cup from the cabinet, ran down the slopping hill and ran up the front brick steps to the house and rang the doorbell. Mr. Thomas came to the door. I could see him through the storm security door. He opened the door and I asked if we could borrow some sugar. He said "sure" and told me to come in. The house had a split foyer, so I entered and stood on the landing at the door. Mr. Thomas went up the few steps to the kitchen to get the sugar. I did not see Mrs. Thomas in her usual spot in the kitchen, so I asked Mr. Thomas where she was and he stated that she was out for the evening. As Mr. Thomas came back down the steps to hand me the sugar, he had this look on his face that made me feel very uncomfortable. He began to move into my personal space on the landing and he held the cup of sugar back from my grasp. I moved backwards toward the storm door and motioned for the door knob. He started to talk and tell me that he had always thought I was a pretty little girl and that I was growing up really fast. I started to thank him for the sugar, hoping that he would hand it to me, but instead he began to unzip my robe and he reached his hand inside and grabbed my innocent little breast and began to move his hand down farther. It happened so fast. I pushed him back onto the steps, the sugar went flying everywhere and ran out the door, crying. I did not know what to think. I was so scared, embarrassed, afraid and confused. What did I do to make Mr. Thomas do that to me? I thought to myself, could he see my body through the robe? Did I say or do something to provoke him? I was too scared to tell my mother, thinking that I did something wrong. I later came to realize that I did absolutely nothing wrong. It was one of the many strategies that the enemy tried to use to destroy me. But, this was only the beginning.

This story may bring rushing memories of your own to the fore front of your mind. It amazes me how many women I have met that have been sexually abused at such a young age. So many woman can probably tell some type of pitch-dark story of the first time they were violated against their will. Whether it was by a neighbor, uncle, cousin or even your mother's boyfriend, it happened! But, I want you to know that you are not alone. The past can be a dark place of no return. At such a young age, seeds of promiscuity, fear and sexual perversion can be planted into the minds of women that soon turn into full-blown sexual acts. Sexual acts that a young lady would have never thought that she would participate in.

Being raised by a single mother, who worked second shift, my siblings and I were left with too much free time to explore our young adventurous, hormonal minds. Where was my father, you ask? That is a good question. He, like many other fathers, only came around when my mother needed us to be disciplined, by the belt of course. The song "Papa was a rolling stone, where ever he laid his hat was his home", could be a good depiction of the father I grew up knowing. So my image of a father was distorted at a very young age. To me, a father was someone who bought you gifts on Christmas, came to take you to church on Easter Sunday, and abused your mother, you and your siblings the rest of the year. He was a person that was truly never around in my younger years to show me the love of a father, respect from the opposite sex, or how I should be treated by a man. I take that back; he did show me how to be treated by a man or rather what was acceptable by a man, and that was abuse.

My starvation for attention, affection and love from the opposite sex drove me into the arms of different young men that were willing to accept me or love me, I thought. So at an early age, I became sexually active. I would not describe myself as a girl that had multiple sex partners or friends with benefits, however I always had a steady boyfriend. Since my mom was never home during after school hours, my boyfriend would just come over after school and hang out. I was responsible for babysitting my younger sister, brother and my niece after school, so I really did not get to enjoy my middle school years. Most kids at this age were involved in school band, sports or other extracurricular school activities. I did not get a chance to attend football or basketball games, like most of my friends, because I had to babysit my siblings. My mom and older sister both worked second shift jobs, so my day went a little something like this. I got up at 6:00am in the morning for school. I got my brother and myself ready for school and then we headed down the hill to the bus stop. When school was over, I could not stay after school to participate in any extracurricular school activities like choir or sports. I had to make sure I got on the school bus and home in time to pick up my sister and niece from the daycare down the street from our house. So at the lovely age of 12, I was driving my mom's grey Granada to the daycare to pick up my sister and niece. Yes, driving I said. Then I had to make sure everyone had something to eat, do chores around the house and do my homework. I loved school. It was my outlet from my life's traumatic events. I was being raised by a single parent mom, who was struggling with a drug addiction. I had a mental and physical abusive father. And I had been sexually molested all before the age of 14 years old. What a life for a pre-teen or teenager. This life definitely made me grow up faster than the average child. I resented the fact, that I could not hang out with my friends and that I was forced to take care of someone else's decision to have children. So I began to rebel. I would have company at the house, when I knew the rules were no company, when my mom was not at home. However, I still let my boyfriend come over. At this age, most teenager's hormones are raging and their minds are curious and so was mine. I felt like I had a boyfriend that loved me, so why not show affection and give in to intimacy. By the summer of my 9th grade year, I found myself in a dilemma that many young women of today face. I got pregnant.

I had been dating, John, for about two and half years. I did not even know I was pregnant. I remember being unusually sleepy. I will never forget how I finally realized I was pregnant. It was at summer Bible camp. I attended Cedine Bible Camp every summer growing up. I absolutely loved Camp Cedine. It was another one of my escape ventures from family life. My siblings and I would go for one week in the summertime. I would always do the Bible studies during the year, so that I could earn my way to camp free of charge. I never wanted to miss camp and I did not want to be a financial burden on my mom. Camp Cedine was where I began to learn about a true relationship with Jesus Christ. We occasionally attended church with my dad, but it was nothing like my experiences at Camp Cedine. During those summer weeks at camp, I would learn Bible verses and scriptures. I learned how to ride horses, swim, and canoe. I even learned how to shoot a rifle. I prided myself on being a sharp shooter every year at camp. One of the great benefits we received at camp was called a snack card. The snack card gave you access to the snack shop, where you could buy candy, chips, pickles and drinks. Well, I never liked pickles until this particular summer. All I wanted from the snack shop was pickles and Kool-Aid. Some of you may remember putting Kool-Aid on your pickle or putting a piece of candy down in your pickle. When this happened, I knew something was wrong. After I returned home from camp, I told my older sister about the Kool-Aid and pickles incident. Since she already had a child, she told me I was probably pregnant. I called my boyfriend, John, and told him. We purchased a pregnancy test from the drug store and sure enough, I was pregnant. John and I were scared and nervous. I knew if my dad found out I was pregnant; he would literally kill me. I was a straight "A" student, on my way to college, with a bright future. I knew my dad would say "I should have never allowed myself to get in such a predicament where I would end up pregnant, when I had my older sister as an example of not to get pregnant." So I did not think I had any other choice, but to have an abortion. John and I started to save for an abortion.

A few weeks had passed and I went to the health clinic and found out that I was about six weeks pregnant. My boyfriend, John, had a part time job, however I was not working. We were not able to save the money fast enough. So I knew I was going to have to tell my parents to get the rest of the money. I remember telling my mom, she was quiet at first, but then her words came as no surprise to me. Her words were exactly what I figured my parents would say. She said, "You know you are not having it." I told her that I knew that and John and I had saved about $200 for the abortion, but needed the remaining amount. Of course, she said that she did not have the remaining money for the abortion and she told my dad. I remember, the look he had on his face when he came over to the house. I was so fearful of my dad. I did not know if he would just beat the baby out of me.

When I said that my dad was abusive, let me give you an example. There was an incident, where I got caught stealing a tube of red lipstick from the old Chattanooga Zayre's Department store. I use to spend most of my summers with my grandmother on the Westside. Going up to Zayre's Department store was one of our summer routine ventures. My cousins, neighborhood friends and I would walk from my grandmother's apartment in the Elks and explore our way through the highway fence that people had made into a shortcut, up the hill to Zarye's. We would look around the store and oooh and aaah over all the pretty clothes and definitely play with all the new toys and electronics. I cannot remember a time that my parents, actually took me shopping for clothes or toys. I do recall my father coming to pick up my siblings and me to go shopping for shoes when we were young, but other than that I do not recall any shopping. Well, we had been ran out of the store before, by the store clerk, for goofing off and being where we should not be, but that did not stop us from going to the department store at least once a week. We knew we had no business being in the department store without adult supervision. Just like a lot of kids without adult supervision and no money to buy anything, my friends would steal stuff all the time. I knew better than to steal, but one day I ignored the morals I had been taught. Being the inquisitive young lady that I was and wanting to wear makeup before it was time, I went and stole that tube of red lipstick. Just when I thought I had gotten away with it, the undercover security officer on duty stopped my friends and me at the front door. I remember feeling embarrassed, scared and petrified of what was about to happen to me. They took us to the back and told us to empty our pockets. Out came the red lipstick and my friend had a Walk-man radio player. My cousin ran and got away. I knew she was going to have to tell my grandmother and she would tell my mom and then my mom would tell my father. The security officer called the police to have us arrested and sent to juvenile. They also called our parents. My mom came to pick me up from the department store. We did not have to ride in the police car nor actually go to juvenile. My mom soon after called and told my dad, the disciplinarian. I was terrified. When it came to getting whippings from my father, he would lecture you for about 30 minutes and then commence to whipping. The lecture part seemed like a lifetime. I hated the lecture part; just whip me and get it over with. On this particular beating, (by the way, my father did not believe in whipping clothes, so you had to strip down to your underwear) he gave me a lecture stating "after this whipping you will never steal again." And believe me I did not. To this day, I still have the marks from the whipping on my legs to prove the harsh beating I received. So when it came to him finding out I was pregnant, I was definitely thinking, the worst beating was going to come from this ordeal.

When my father came to the house to see me after my mom delivered the displeasing news, he had a look of disappointment and anger upon his face as I watched him get out of the car. I always tried to please my father, by having good grades and staying out of trouble, but I could not imagine what he would do in this case. I thought I would meet him outside in the yard where there were a lot of witnesses of kids playing instead of being inside the house by myself with him. We stood by the car, me with my head down and him with those beady eyes staring right through me. He began to tell me that he was very disappointed in me and that there was no way that I was going to have this child, because I was going to college and going to make something of myself. He gave the rest of the money to my mom for the abortion and left.

I was alright with having the abortion, until it was time to actually go to the clinic. My grandmother had to take me because my mother was working. I remember my grandmother pulling into the driveway and me coming out of the house, I suddenly became very sick. I began to throw up before I could even get in the car. I remember my grandmother asking me if I was ok, but that was the jest of her conversation. I threw up from my house all the way to the abortion clinic. My grandmother had to pull over several times. But never once did she tell me that I did not have to have this abortion. No one told me that I had another choice. In this day and age, there are women service clinics and centers that teach young women that they have options, like giving the baby up for adoption, but I do not recall anyone giving me options. When I arrived at the abortion clinic off of Lee Hwy, I remember entering the clinic by myself. I filled out some paperwork and waited for my name to be called. When they called my name, I went into this room, where I was instructed by the nurse to get undressed, climb onto the table, lie back on the table and the doctor would be in the room in a moment. I closed my eyes and I remember the vacuum and suction sounds. It was all over in about 15 minutes. The nurse told me to rise up, she gave me a pad, some cleansing wipes and instructed me to go into this room and get dressed. The doctor and the nurse left the room and I began to cry and think I just killed my son. I remember seeing this fleshy tissue on my jellies (shoe like sandals) and I cried even harder. I cleaned myself up and got dressed. I went to the front of the clinic to check out. I was given a sheet with some instructions on it on how to handle any pain or heavy bleeding and a prescription. My grandmother drove me back home. I remember sleeping a lot that day and then I was awakened by sharp pains. I rushed to the bathroom and I was bleeding so heavy with lots of blood clots that it scared me. So I ran to tell my mother and I remember her saying, "What do you want me to do? I'll go and get the prescription filled that they gave you and there are some extra pads under the sink." I felt so alone. From that day forward, no one ever mentioned anything else about the abortion. It was like it never happened, but years later in my life, the memories would return.

One may ask, "How do you get over such a traumatic event? I thought it would be through time and school. But today, I know better. I was young, so I eventually went back to school and healed physically from the surgery. John and I broke up shortly after the abortion. I believe deep down inside he resented the fact that I had the abortion, even though no one ever said, "You Do Not Have to Have an Abortion." Not John, my older sister, parents, grandmother, no one. I tried my best to forget what I had done with my child and focused more on what my parents said I needed to do; "make something of myself."

PRAYER

Lord, I pray for my sister today, that she will be able to forgive herself of the past. That she knows that the past no longer has any bondage or chains holding her back from her destiny. I pray against the spirit of shame, guilt, and fear. I pray that my sister will forgive all those that have despitefully sinned against her. Let her forgive all her abusers, whether they are a stranger, family or friend. I pray for strength, power and a sound mind. I pray that my sister will face her past and acknowledge that it was not her fault and move forward with purpose and destiny in her heart and mind. I pray that my sister will forget those things that are behind and press toward the mark of a higher calling in Christ Jesus. May the Lord comfort you and keep you as you accept the past and use it as a stepping stone to thrust you into your destiny. I pray for peace, love and joy to guard your heart, mind and your soul. May the angels of heaven take charge over you. May you feel the Lord's presence at all times. For He will never leave you or forsake you. You were not alone during these dark and traumatic times and you are not alone now. You are a survivor!

EMPOWERMENT CONFESSIONS

Not that I have already obtained it or have already become perfect, but I press on so that I may lay hold of that for which also I was laid hold of by Christ Jesus. Brethren, I do not regard myself as having laid hold of it yet; but one thing I do: forgetting what lies behind and reaching forward to what lies ahead, I press on toward the goal for the prize of the upward call of God in Christ Jesus.
Philippians 3:12-14

For I know that this will turn out for my deliverance through your prayers and the provision of the Spirit of Jesus Christ.
Philippians 1:19

Even though I walk through the valley of the shadow of death, I fear no evil, for You are with me; Your rod and Your staff, they comfort me.
Psalms 23:4

Peace I leave with you; My peace I give to you; not as the world gives do I give to you. Do not let your heart be troubled, nor let it be fearful.
John 14:27

PART ONE: THE PITCH-DARK
THE RESCUE SYNDROME

"You're going to come across people in your life that say all the right things at the right times. But in the end, it's always their actions you should judge them by. It's actions, not words, that matter."
— Nicholas Sparks, The Rescue

As I entered into my sophomore year of school, my home life was still in disarray. My older sister was in the process of graduating and moving out of the house, so that left me as the oldest sibling in the house. I had come into the realization, that my mother was smoking more than just marijuana. This is when crack and cocaine became real to me. You may remember those drug commercials back in the late 80's that showed an egg frying as a symbol of your brain on drugs. Well, this is what I thought about my mom when I would see her free base crack. I learned later in my life that she was trying to run away from the divorce of my father. And my dad was the one who introduced her to drugs in the first place. My mom tried to be the best provider that she could be without my father around or helping as much. She always made sure we had food in the refrigerator to eat, even though it was a lot of bologna, hot dogs, chili and red Kool-Aid. I believe this is the reason I do not eat bologna and hot dogs to this day, plus it is horrible food for the body. My mother made sure she kept the electricity on in the house, which provided heat in the winter and cool air in the summer. Other than the basic necessities to live as a child, we did not receive any extra loving care. I remember my mom would sometimes order us pizza from Pizza Hut on Fridays, when she wanted us out of her hair. She would then disappear into her bedroom with the door shut. I remember her coming out her bedroom and going back and forth to the stove. Then she would begin to start looking for something on the floor. I would go to her room and peek through the crack in the door and watch how her demeanor changed. Her eyes would get bucked out, and she would be biting her lip. She would be down on the floor looking at every little piece of white lint, paper or trash. I later found out this is what it looks like when you get high by free basing crack. I hated this look. It was as if she was paranoid about everything. She also had this horrible boyfriend that she got high with. She got high with the neighbors and my play auntie that lived across the street. They would come in and out of the house all the time when they were getting high. She was what you would call a functioning addict. She paid the bills and made sure my siblings and I had something to eat, but she checked out the remainder of the time, especially on the weekends.

I remember one horrible Saturday morning. I would always climb in the bed with my mother on Saturday mornings to cuddle and watch cartoons while she slept, or sometimes we would talk. I just wanted to be next to her. My mom was a very compassionate, loving mother, and even today, she still is. Always willing to help someone. Well, this Saturday morning there would be no cuddling, just fear, anger, disappointment, resentment and crying. As I entered my mother's room and turned on the television, she sat up in the bed and told me no television this morning. As I turned to ask why, I saw my mother's face as the sunlight shone through the opening in the red curtains in her bed room. I gasped at the sight and asked her what happened. Her face looked like the elephant man. Her eye was black and swollen to where her right eye was practically shut. Her lip was busted and swollen. She had bruises up and down her arm. She had a knot on her head. I rushed to her side, trying to be brave and hold back the tears, and stated that we needed to get her to the hospital. But the look in her eyes told me that this was not an option. Because if she could have gone to the doctor, she would have already gone. This was an outcome of one of her weekend drug escapades. She had been beat up by a drug pusher the night before while she was out trying to buy crack. This is when my sadness turned to anger and disappointment because she could not go to the hospital to get help due to the events that led to her injuries. She could not tell the doctor that she was out buying crack, which is an illegal drug, and was beaten up by a drug dealer; then she would be in trouble. I remember holding her face in my hands and looking straight at her and saying, "Are you going to let drugs kill you?" She did not respond. From that day forward, I began to resent my mother, and I lost a lot of respect for her. It was as if I became very numb when it came to our relationship. I could not understand why she would not stop using drugs. Why would she put my siblings and me in harm's way? I wanted to leave our house; it became a living nightmare.

I soon realized that this would be the norm in my life. No father and really no mother at times. So at a very young age, about 14, I started working. My older sister and I forged our birth certificates to make it seem as if we were a year older than we truly were, so that we could go to work. I always wanted to have more than just hand me downs for clothes or just better looking clothes and shoes. So this was the way to get those things because they were not going to come from my parents. By the age of 16, I became a shift manager at Burger King. I loved to work, so my life consisted of work and going to school. These were my escape locations from the real world I was living in at home.

I desired to have a normal life, like I thought many of my school mates were experiencing in their teenage years. I remember one summer, being at home and watching TV with my neighbors' son, Keith. He lived on the other side of our duplex in apartment B. We attended school together and he often came over, especially in the summertime. Keith was an only child. He was a couple of years older than I. It was nothing for me to have on shorts and a pajama gown when he was around. He was like a big brother, like family. My mom and his mom hung out, and he came over to the house to eat a lot. However, this summer would change all this hanging out. In my house, we used to have these clear plastic runners in our living room, so that we didn't track up the carpet. I remember Keith and I were watching cartoons or something meaningless. It was still rather early for a summer day for me. I always slept late in the summertime, so it was probably between noontime and 1:00 o'clock. I would lay on the runners on the carpet with a blanket, because the runners would cool me off in the summertime; they were always cold from the air. I had no warning or sign of what was about to happen next. My younger brother and sister must have been outside and my mother at work, I guess, because no one was in the house with us. Before I knew it, right in the middle of a commercial, Keith was on top of me trying to get my shorts down. I remember screaming and hollering, saying, "What are you doing?" I was kicking and trying to fight him off of me, and I slipped and slid on that cold runner on top of that blanket. He managed to get my shorts down and he began to press up against me with his private parts. Just as he tried to penetrate my private area, I managed to knee him in the groin area. He fell over, I got up and ran to what we called the small bathroom in our little duplex and locked the door. I was so afraid that he would pull the door open and continue to try to rape me. I stayed in that bathroom for what seemed like a lifetime. I remember hearing the front door shut and my little sister calling for me. I finally came out the bathroom. She asked me where I had been, and I told her that I'd been there all the time. This summer left me scared and wondering if I did something to provoke Keith to do something like that to me. We used to walk home up the hill from the school bus stop together. From then on, I made sure that I got off the school bus before he did and walked with some of the other kids up the hill to our house. He avoided me like the plague. We never spoke again after that summer. Shortly after, he and his mother moved away and

I was glad. I was always scared he would break into our house and try to finish the job, since the door to our house never really locked. It had to have been the Lord that protected my siblings and me; because you could just push hard on our front door, and it would just come right open, even if it was locked. I remember I would put chairs under the doorknob at night sometimes, when I was scared.

I still longed for a relationship with the opposite sex; since I did not grow up with a healthy balance of love from my father. I found myself looking for love in all the wrong places. And then, here comes the love of my life, Howard, or so I thought. Howard was tall, brown and handsome. He had a beautiful smile and was normally quiet. He was funny, and many people genuinely liked him. He had this certain way about himself. He was well respected at the high school. He played the drums in the marching band; back then you were kind of "hot" if you played on the drum line. But, he also had a bad side to him. He was in a group called the Nikes. All the girls wanted to date someone in the Nikes group, at least my girlfriends, which were few. The Nike's were the group to be in if you were at our high school, Brainerd High. The guys were well known by many around the city. I met Howard working at Burger King. I knew him from school as well. We were both dating someone else at the time, when we began to flirt with each other at the restaurant. We both worked the late shift and he would offer to take me home, when my mother or sister could not pick me up from work. He was very nice to me in the beginning. He gave me a feeling of being protected when I was with him. I do not remember if he really asked me to be his girlfriend; I do remember we just seemed to be together more and more everyday. He broke up with his girlfriend first. Then I eventually left the guy I was going with at the time. Howard and I were inseparable. We went to school together, and I would go over to his house after school most of the time when we did not have to go to work. There was nothing that Howard would not do for me. He would give me money when I needed it for clothes or take me out to eat. We went out of town together, like to Atlanta Six Flags Amusement Park or Myrtle Beach, just to get away. I truly thought Howard was the best thing that had ever happened to me. I remember, vividly, when I came to the realization that he was the one I truly wanted to marry.

Since I was no longer going home right after school, my younger brother, who is 2 years younger than I, was left with the responsibility of watching our younger sister. I was supposed to go home to watch both of them, but sometimes I would tell my brother to just page me if they needed something. One day, I received a page from my brother telling me to call home, quickly. When I called home, he told me to come home. Our dad had made a surprise visit and found my younger sister and him alone. My dad wanted to know where I was since it was way after the time I should be home. So I hurried home in my grey Granada car that my mom had finally given me to drive. Of course, I was at Howard's house. I told him what was going on at my house and that I would call him later, once my dad left. Remember, my dad did not live with us at all. He was only known as the disciplinarian. I do not know if my mom called him. I just knew it was not going to go well when I got home. Even as I got older, I was still very fearful of my father. As I entered our two bedroom duplex, he was sitting in the living room. I walked into the house and began to straighten things up in the house. I went to the kitchen to wash up the dishes, and he followed me into the kitchen and began to ask questions. He asked, "Where have you been?" I told him that I was at a friend's house. He asked, "Why are your brother and sister home by themselves, and it is dark outside?" I told him that I had been in touch with them, and everything was ok. He then began to raise his voice and yell as usual about how they were not old enough to watch themselves no matter what I thought. He proceeded to back me into a corner of the kitchen. I began to look around to see what I could use to protect myself if he attempted to hit me. I warned him not to put his hands on me. I was about 17 years old, at this time. I told him that he had no right to try and whip me or hit me since he was not the parent that raised me. He commanded me to shut up and he would do as he damn well pleased; I was still his child. I told him if he hit me, I was going to call the police. I then yelled at my brother who was watching from a distance to go next door and call the police first, and then call mom at work and tell her what was going on. You, see my mom had taken out a restraining order on my dad because of his abusive behavior towards us and my mom. My dad threatened my brother not to move, or he would get a whipping as well. My brother was petrified. I told him to run and take our younger sister with him. I instructed him not to come back to the house from the neighbors, until he saw the police pull up in the driveway. My brother and sister ran next door. I commenced to tell my father if he touched me, I would do whatever I needed to do to protect myself. My father raised his hand and slapped me and I fell back into the dish drain on the counter. I picked up a knife and warned him that if he hit me again I would use the knife that was in my hand. I told him that he had no right to come to our house, anytime he got ready, and abuse us. He gave me the most evil look. I did not know what he was going to do, but I knew what I was going to do if he hit me again. He turned to leave knowing, if he was there when the police arrived he would be in trouble. As soon as my dad left, I called Howard and he immediately came to my rescue. My mom also arrived shortly after my dad left. I told her what happened. My mom stayed with my brother and sister, and I left with Howard. Howard told me that I would never have to put up with my dad hitting me again. All I had to do was call him, and he would take care of me. Howard, my rescuer, my hero, my protector. He would take me out of all the troubles and bad situations that I would experience in that two bedroom duplex, I knew as my home. He was my way out.

After that incident, I was glued to Howard every waking moment. I began to spend a lot of time at his house. Long days we spent together, way into the morning hours when we were out of school for the summer especially. Whatever he wanted me to do, I did it.

We went to prom together, his prom and mine. Anytime he wanted sex, I was there to give it to him. I loved him, and this was my way of letting him know that I did. Since my mom was still using drugs and my younger siblings were old enough to watch themselves, I rarely went home after school anymore. Howard's family accepted me with open arms. Howard was a couple of years older than I, so he graduated before I did. And right before I graduated from high school, he proposed to me with a 1-carat marquise diamond. Howard was on his way into the army, and he wanted to make sure I would be there waiting for him when he got back from basic training. I know this seems like a dream come true, but remember I said that Howard had a bad side too.

During the years that we were dating, Howard was very jealous. At first I thought it was kind of cute that he did not want any other guys talking to me, but things soon got out of hand. Any time he caught a guy looking at me, Howard would threaten them and me. Before Howard graduated from high school, he got into some trouble with the law. Being a part of the Nike group had its challenges. One day I noticed that Howard had way more money than what he was making at Burger King. I remember being at his house, when the police came to arrest him. I did not know what was going on, but I soon found out that he and some of the others in the Nike group had been kicking people's doors in and robbing them. He would take the stolen goods and sell it at pawn shops for money. This arrest got Howard a criminal record. When he was released from jail for this offense, he tried to sell drugs and I was totally against this. I saw what drugs did to my family, and I was not about to be a part of it. I threatened to leave him, so he quit the drug selling. However, he was caught by the police with drugs in his car. These criminal offenses followed him into basic training for the military, even after the army recruiter told him that he could still enlist with these charges. To his disappointment, he was kicked out of the army and sent back home, the summer before I went to college. Howard was devastated and angry at the world. He began to take out this anger on me. He did not want me to go anywhere with my friends, and when I would, he would show up and embarrass me. He began to yell and scream at me just like my dad. The verbal abuse soon progressed into physical abuse.

I remember working two jobs the summer before I went to college, to try and save some money for school. My day job was at the Senior Living, and then I worked third shift at the Conoco gas station. Howard would come down and sit with me at night sometime, since the gas station was in a bad area of city. One morning when I was getting off from work, instead of going to Howard's grandmother's house where he lived, I went over to my mom's house to visit and I fell asleep. I did not hear my pager going off several times throughout the day, so when I finally woke up late that afternoon, Howard had paged me about 20 times. I tried to call him back at his grandmother's house, but she informed me that he was not there. I quickly drove over to Howard's house because I knew he would be furious that I did not call him back from all his pages. By the time I arrived, Howard was at home. I entered the house and spoke with Howard's grandmother and aunt. His aunt began to say, "You know you are in trouble. Howard has been looking for you all day." I told her I had fallen asleep over my mom's house. I proceeded to Howard's bedroom, which was located in the back of the house. As I walked in, Howard shut the door behind me and locked the door. He began to question me about where I had been all day. I explained to him that I had fallen asleep over at my mom's house, but he did not believe me. He began to throw me from wall to wall. He called me all kinds of names and told me that I was lying. He accused me of laying up with another man. I tried to get out of the room and away from him, but he kept choking me and pushing me down on the bed. I was afraid that he would kill me. His grandmother came to the bedroom and told Howard to leave me alone and open the door, but he ignored her. He had the look of the devil in his eyes, just like my dad would have when he was whipping us. I realized that day I was with someone just like my dad. Howard threw me on the bed again and climbed on top of me and began to choke the life out of me. I believe the only reason he let go was because I began to turn blue from the loss of oxygen. I finally got away from him by throwing a bottle of rubbing alcohol in his face. As he was hollering from the alcohol burning his eyes, I managed to climb out the bedroom window and run to my car. It seemed like I was in that bedroom with him beating me for hours. I went to mom's house and cried myself to sleep. As I was driving, I was thinking, "What had I done to make him so angry?" How much longer could I stand our relationship this way? But abuse was all I knew. It was all I had seen in relationships of the opposite sex. I really thought this was how married couples, all over the world, got along. One day they fight, then the next day they make up and move on with the relationship. So when Howard called to apologize later on that night; I forgave him again. These types of incidents became the norm for our relationship and I accepted it. Howard was my savior, my provider, and my protector from my family issues.

Sadly, this is the norm for a lot of young woman in relationships, whether during their teenage years or later in life. You may be one of them. It could be a part of your past, or you may be in it right now. You might be wondering and thinking, "How am I going to get out?" I am here to tell you that you can get out. You were not created to be anyone's punching bag. It is not love. It is a device of the enemy to kill, steal and destroy your life. It is a generational curse. Today you must leave and tell someone what is going on. Enough is enough. You deserve so much more, and God has so much more in store for your life. God has a plan for your life and it is for good and not evil. You can do it. Leave this abusive relationship now! This book will give you the strength and courage to move past your fears into a new chapter of your life.

The stigma of rape, being abused, of being powerless, leaves a person wanting to regain her sense of control over her life. Being enslaved to abuse sometimes feels hopeless with no way out. This is exactly what the abuser wants you to feel hopeless, confused and blinded by darkness of his/her lies from the truth. You may be thinking, "What darkness and roughness must a person experience to become the light of its destiny, a true diamond." Just as I experienced many dark situations, the making of diamond has similar situations that it has to go through to become the true value of its worth, as well. Diamonds actually start off as a black piece of charcoal, deep down where no one dares to venture. However it becomes the most beautiful jewel that man has ever seen. As a woman in the making of a rare jewel, you must press onward and upward out of pitch-dark situations where you have no control. You must push past all the rock and rough places to become the diamond you were destined to be. As a diamond is lifted from the bottom of the volcanic blackness, its journey is really only beginning. So was my journey of self-discovery and worth.

PRAYER

Lord, I pray strength, courage and confidence for my sister today. I pray that she realizes that she no longer has to stay in an abusive relationship. I pray for people and resources for my sister to move out of the same house with the abuser and go forward in her singleness. I pray against every negative word spoken over her life. My sister, you are fearfully and wonderfully made. You are created in the image and likeness of the creator, God. I pray that the anointing of God breaks every generational curse of abuse, low self-esteem and feelings of unworthiness. I pray you will recognize that God is calling you to higher heights and deeper depths into His love. No one can love you unless they know who created love and that is God. God is love. God has a plan for your life. A plan to prosper you and bring you to an expected end of goodness. I pray as you leave this relationship, that great and mighty things happen in your life. You can do this. You can start over. Remember you are never alone.

EMPOWERMENT CONFESSIONS

For I know the plans I have for you," says the Lord. "They are plans for good and not for disaster, to give you a future and a hope.
Jeremiah 29:11

For You formed my inward parts; You wove me in my mother's womb. I will give thanks to You, for I am fearfully and wonderfully made; Wonderful are Your works, And my soul knows it very well.
Psalms 139:13-14

"I will never leave you nor forsake you."
Hebrews 13:5

I can do all things through Christ who strengthens me.
Philippians 4:13

Yet in all these things we are more than conquerors through Him
who loved us.
Romans 8:37

PART TWO: THE PRESSURE
BEING ON THE YARD – IT'S GETTING HOT IN HERE!

When we long for life without difficulties, remind us that oaks grow strong in contrary winds and diamonds are made under pressure.
-Peter Marshall

Finally, I was leaving home on my way to college at the University of Tennessee, Knoxville (UTK). I did not know much about UTK, except that it had a great engineering program. Growing up, I always dreamed that I would attend the elite Spelman College. However, when I visited Spelman while I was still in high school, I thought to myself, "I'm not going to spend all my money to go to a private college where the campus grounds reminded me of the projects back home." The dorms and buildings looked run down. Nothing liked I dreamed or expected. So when a classmate from my high school asked me to be her roommate at UTK, I said ok. My parents did not really provide any direction as to what school I should attend for college or what field of study I should pursue. Again, they were consumed with their own lives. The only advice my mother gave me was, "We do not have any money and we are poor, so you will qualify for all the financial aid that you need to go to school." Also they both, meaning my parents, had the demand that I was definitely going to college to make something of myself. I knew that I loved math and my father was an electrical engineer who worked for TVA and made a lot of money. So I thought, why not pursue engineering myself? If my dad could do it, so could I.

I graduated from high school and ranked 10th in my class. I was a straight "A" student for the majority of my school years. I practically could have applied to any school, if I would have had a little adult direction. Even though I had no real direction from family, I was always more mature than most people who were my age. I was very strong-willed, resourceful and determined in high school, so maybe my parents did not think I needed any help getting ready for college. I applied to the colleges that my other smart classmates applied too. To my surprise, I received a full scholarship to University of Tennessee Chattanooga and Tennessee State University, but I did not want to stay anywhere near home, so UTC was definitely out of the question. TSU was an all-black college, and I thought I would never learn anything there, so I opted for the partial scholarship offered from UTK in their engineering program.

My relationship with Howard was going as strong as it could be, in spite of our ups and downs. He was not thrilled that I was going to college, but very supportive. Our plan was I would go to college, complete my degree and we would be married right after I graduated. Being the good student that I've always been, I began to delve into my studies for engineering. I embraced my new college life, making new friends and getting to know the city of Knoxville. Even though I was at college with a sense of new freedom and away from the troubles at home, including Howard, I still remained faithful and loyal to our plan. My roommate and I were very homesick the first semester of school, and we went home every weekend. This helped my relationship with Howard. Soon, my roommate's parents could not afford to come and pick us up every weekend, so things began to get really heated between Howard and me.

I call college life the "devil's den." You have a young teenager, age 18, with no rules, no curfew, and nobody telling you when to wake up or go to class. You have your own room or apartment and all the freedom that a teenager could ever want. This combination spells trouble all the way. Staying on campus on the weekends, left me with a lot of time on my hands. So I began to go to the Greek parties and clubs with my new friends. I loved to dance, so parties were my thing to do. I had never taken a drink of liquor before my college days. And guess what, I could not hold my liquor down, as some would say either. If there was party on campus, then my friends and I were there. This type of lifestyle soon began to take a toll on my grades and put pressure on my relationship with Howard back home. As I mentioned earlier, I was a straight "A" student. I never really had to study in high school to maintain good grades. Obviously, this was not going to work in college. I found myself failing in the engineering program. And things with Howard were getting worse as each day passed.

Since I was not able to go home on the weekends, Howard and I would talk on the phone long distance for hours and accumulate huge phone bill charges, that neither of us could afford to pay. This was back in the day when you had to pay for long distance calls from state to state. So I suggested we limit our phone calls, and this made Howard very angry. He began to accuse me of sleeping around on him while I was in college. No matter how many times I told him this was not true and that I loved him only, he did not believe me. When I did get to go home and spent time with him, sometimes he would be abusive verbally and physically. I would say to myself, "He just misses me and thinks that I am cheating on him, so I need to show him how much I love him." So I would have sex with him anytime he wanted, how he wanted it and anywhere he wanted it. I was definitely living a sexually active life with Howard since he was going to be my husband anyway. But this was not enough. I would tell myself, "Once we get married, things are going to be different. Howard is going to change, and we are going to have a perfect marriage if I could just make it to graduation with a degree." However, if I did not get myself together with my grades, I was not going to graduate.

My sophomore year in college, I switched my major quickly. I lost my partial scholarship from failing in the engineering program. Since I loved math, I switched to Business Finance and Accounting, and things became real easy to me again. I could party all weekend and still make "A's". This was the right move for me. I was continually trying to hold things together with Howard, until he was sentenced to do time in prison.

When Howard was sent home from the army, he got into trouble with the law for selling drugs. So when I went to college he had a pending court date for this offense. I assured him that no matter what happened in court, I would remain by his side. Well, his day in court came and Howard was sentenced to do 11 months and 29 days. This really put a strain on our relationship. Howard's verbal abuse got worse. When he called me from prison, he said things like, "I know you are sleeping around on me. I hope you get AIDS and die." Well, I finally had enough of the accusations. I broke off the engagement with Howard. So for the rest of my sophomore year, I began to date other guys I met in college.

One guy that is worth an honorable mention is Crook. I know it's a strange name, but it was his nickname. We met when I started working at the Krystal's on the strip in Knoxville. From first glance, he was definitely not the typical tall, dark and handsome man I was used to dating; however, he was persistent when it came to asking me out on a date. I was so hurt by Howard that I really did not want to enter into another relationship, but finally I gave in to Crook. He was like a breath of fresh air compared to my relationship with Howard. He was fun to be with and very witty in numerous ways. He could always make me laugh and smile. He would wine and dine me. He was truly a gentleman at all times. I knew that Crook really cared for me; however, I could not fully give my heart to him because it was still with Howard. Crook was like my rebound guy. Someone to take the place of Howard since he was incarcerated.

However, I made some huge mistakes with Crook. I moved off campus for a short time and moved into an apartment with him. I bought furniture for the apartment with my credit. I also was sexually intimate with Crook, without using no protection. We were so sexually intimate that I would buy pregnancy tests all the time, especially when they had a sale, "buy one and get the second one free". When I think about all these things, how ridiculous was I. Crook and I had a lot of things in common. We liked to dance, drink, get high and watch sports. We became great friends during the year or so we dated. I finally came to my senses, a little, and moved out of the apartment with Crook and moved in with a close friend of mine, Trina. Trina was like a mother and a sister to me. She allowed me to live with her, rent free for the rest of my junior and senior years in college. She would cook for Crook and me. She would make my favorite meal: roast, macaroni & cheese, collard greens and cornbread. We were truly like family. Crook and I became god parents to Trina's son, Meke. I really enjoyed being able to experience her having my god-son in hospital. This time in my life seemed so sweet. Crook asked me to marry him several times, but I was not ready. A part of me really contemplated spending the rest of my life with Crook. However, phone calls and letters from Howard about him being released from prison quickly changed those feelings.

My college life was clearly off the chain. I did whatever I wanted to do whether it was good for me or not. College life was where I was introduced to alcohol and drugs. I took my first sip of liquor and smoked my first joint in college. I was having sexual intercourse without protection, like AIDS had not hit the scene. It was only God's hand upon my life that I did not get pregnant or get a sexually transmitted disease. Being in the hot devil's den seemed fun at the time, but the residual effects were not to be desired.

One will never know the true love and power of the creator's hand upon your life during the process of making you into a rare jewel. Especially, when you are living such a self-centered and self-indulgent life as I did in college. This process is like being on a potter's wheel. The clay cannot say to the potter that I have no need of you. The potter has the ultimate vision for the clay. True diamonds must endure extreme heat to form the crystallization we see every day in diamonds. So if you are reading this book and your college life was similar to mine, or if you are getting ready to go into college, know that the Father's hand is upon your life. He will take all your heated situations and use them for your good.

PRAYER

Lord, I pray for the teenager that is on her way to college, and she feels that she has no real direction from parents or wise counsel. I pray that you will lead someone across her path before college, that she will not ignore, who will engrave purpose and vision in her mind. I pray for a Kingdom church family for her in college that will encourage her and teach her to keep and apply your moral law to her life. I pray that she does not get swept away by the hype and sense of freedom of being in college. I pray that she is focused and determined to remain pure, holy and blameless before you. I pray that she has decided her choice of study before she enters college. I pray that she will know her purpose and identity lies in Christ. I pray against the enemy's devices, schemes and plans. They shall not prosper. I pray that she will not be entangled with sin. I pray that she will take the way of escape when she finds herself falling into temptation. I pray a hedge of protection around her heart, mind and her body. You were created to succeed, to move forward, and to make an impact. I pray for wise counsel from professors, co-workers, and advisors. May they lead you with the unction of the Holy Spirit. If you fall, then get up, confess your sins to your Heavenly Father and change your friends and associations. Do not be deceived, birds of a feather flock together. Lord, I pray that you will join her with friends of the same caliber. I pray that your college life with be filled with joy, laughter, peace and love. You are in the Father's hand and nothing can separate you from the love of the Father.

EMPOWERMENT CONFESSIONS

Do not be deceived: "Bad company corrupts good morals."
I Corinthians 15:33

No weapon that is formed against you will prosper.
Isaiah 54:17

No temptation has overtaken you but such as is common to man; and
God is faithful, who will not allow you to be tempted beyond what
you are able, but with the temptation will provide the way of escape
also, so that you will be able to endure it.
Your body is the temple.
I Corinthians 10:13

Let us hold fast the confession of our faith without wavering, for He
who promised is faithful; and let us consider how to stimulate one
another to love and good deeds, not forsaking our own assembling
together, as is the habit of some, but encouraging one another; and
all the more as you see the day drawing near.
Hebrews 10:23-25

For I am convinced that neither death, nor life, nor angels, nor
principalities, nor things present, nor things to come, nor powers, nor
height, nor depth, nor any other created thing, will be able to
separate us from the love of God, which is in Christ Jesus our Lord.
Romans 8:38-39

A wise man will hear and increase in learning,
And a man of understanding will acquire wise counsel.
Proverbs 1:5

The fear of the Lord is the beginning of knowledge;
Fools despise wisdom and instruction. Proverbs 1:7

PART TWO: THE PRESSURE
TRYING TO HANG ON TO WHAT I THOUGHT WAS
MR. RIGHT

We must be willing to let go of the life we have planned, so as to
accept the life that has been prepared for us.
-Frenise Mann

Seeing Howard's face again after we had been apart for over a year,
made my heart flutter. He looked so good to me. He was more
muscular than before, since he had all that free time in prison to lift
weights. I journeyed home to visit him the weekend that he was
released. He had written to me and asked if I would come and see
him. I was in my senior year in college with about nine months left
before graduation. When I arrived at his grandmother's house, he
met me at the front door. He was smiling from ear to ear, and he
grabbed me up into his huge arms and held me so tight. I rested my
head on his chest and inhaled his cologne like I would do when we
were together. I thought I was going to melt in his arms. The
memories of how things used to be between us when we first met
came rushing back to my mind. How he protected me from my
family issues and provided for me when I was in need. It felt like the
good old times. He kissed my neck and whispered in my ear that he
missed me so much and wanted to make things right between us.
When he finally stopped hugging me and put me back on my feet, I
was hooked again. Of course, I slept with Howard that night, and I
was convinced that he had changed. I was convinced that things

would be different this time. It is amazing how sex can really fog up your brain from the truth.

If I was going to be back with Howard, then that meant I would have to break up with Crook when I went back to campus. As I was driving back to Knoxville, I replayed the awesome weekend that I had spent with Howard. I was also trying to figure out how I was going to tell Crook that I was going back to Howard. I knew that Crook had always feared that I would go back to Howard, no matter how many times I assured him I would not. Crook knew the truth about me and my feelings for Howard. I really did not want to hurt Crook, so I did not prolong the news.

Crook was definitely hurt when I told him that Howard and I were getting back together. However, he still wanted to remain friends. In fact too close of a friend. He made it a point to continue to wine and dine me during the week while I was at school and I let him. Crook was the one that made me laugh, and we had gotten to be good friends besides the intimate part of our relationship. It did not help that Crook and I still drank and hung out together occasionally, which led to erotic actions afterwards. So I found myself trying to build my relationship back with Howard in Chattanooga and staying out of the sheets with Crook while I was in Knoxville. The things that I said I would never do, like sleeping with two guys during the same season of life, is exactly what I found myself caught up in. I knew I was wrong, but I did not have the self-control to stop.

Howard proposed to me for the second time, and things seemed to be going well. He was still very jealous, and the abuse started all over again. I told myself that things would be different once we got married. I only had about five months left to graduate. I decided to get my life right with God. My friend Trinia and I found a church that we both enjoyed. I stopped doing some of the things that I knew was wrong, like drinking alcohol and going to parties. I realized this was not what I wanted out of life. Plus it was always the same people, doing the same thing, going nowhere. It was as if I looked around and saw all the people I started college with graduating, and the ones that were there when I started college were still there. I also stopped sleeping around with Crook. I had to resist temptations on several occasions; however, I was ready to be totally faithful to Howard. I was determined to make it down the altar with Howard, and we would live happily ever after.

The "happily ever after" turned into a horror movie. Anytime I was with Howard, it turned into an argument. I knew deep down inside something was wrong. He began to accuse me of sleeping around on him again. Anytime we were out in public, he was always watching to see if guys were looking at me and he practically dared anyone to talk to me. I remember an incident when we were out on a date at the bowling alley. We were walking down the foyer, and a guy grabbed me to give me a hug and speak. I immediately pulled away so as not to make a scene. The guy started playing saying, "Don't act like you don't remember me?" I got real nervous because I could feel Howard's eyes on me; waiting for my response. I am so horrible with remembering names, but I never forget a face. Everything in my mind and body was trying to remember where I knew this guy from, and I could not recall. I knew that Howard was getting more furious by the minute. Before I knew it, Howard had grabbed the guy by his neck and slung him into the wall. He began to tell the guy "Keep your hands off of my women." At that very moment, before Howard punched him in the face, I remembered the guy from a Greek party back in college. I explained to Howard that I did not have any relations with this guy, and that he was a friend of a friend back on campus. Howard let the guy go and he ran for his life. Of course, Howard cussed me out and dragged me to the car. I was so embarrassed, that I did not show my face in that bowling alley for a long time. Howard did apologize, but he did not stop his accusations against me. I started to suspect that Howard must be seeing someone else besides me, because his jealousy and indictments of me cheating on him had gone to another level. I did all in my power to please Howard to show him that I only wanted to be with him, to marry him. Even to the point that I began to drive back and forth from Knoxville to Chattanooga every day to be with him after my classes were over. He told me that he needed me back in Chattanooga with him every day. I would plead with him that I only had a couple more months before graduation, and then I would be home permanently. He still was not satisfied. So I decided to take a road trip home one weekend to surprise Howard. But something on the inside of me told me that I would be the one who was surprised.

As I was driving down the road, I remember praying to God that he would give me the strength to be able to handle whatever I was about to see when I arrived at Howard's home. It seemed as if the drive took longer than the usual 1 hour and 15 minutes for me. It was as if my heart was racing the entire time I was driving home. Deep down inside, I knew that Howard was seeing someone else; I just did not have any proof. I had seen several red flags, but up to this point, I had ignored them all.

As I pulled up in front of Howard's grandmother's house, where he resided, a blue Ford Taurus I had never seen before was parked on the side of the house. My heart sank because I knew someone was in the house with him besides his relatives. I knocked on the door and Howard's uncle greeted me at the door. I asked where Howard was located, and he stated "Upstairs." I entered the house, sat down on the couch and chit-chatted with Howard's grandmother, Ms. Joy. She was very dear to my heart, especially since the passing of my grandmother on my father's side of the family. She was doing her usual Friday night ritual: smoking a cigarette, drinking coffee and watching wrestling. I asked her where Howard was as well, and she stated upstairs in his bedroom. I must have talked with Ms. Joy for about 20-30 minutes. She did not warn me or tell me anything before I embarked upon the steps to Howard's bedroom. I kissed her on the cheek and proceeded to the back of the house where the steps were located to Howard's bedroom upstairs.

I started up the stairs, and as I reached midway, I could see a little girl sitting on the floor on top of some pillows, and a woman sitting behind her on the bed combing the little girl's hair. As I approached the top of the stairs, I saw Howard lying across the bed watching television. I tried to remain calm and not make a scene and disrespect Ms. Joy's home. So I greeted everyone in the room and proceeded to walk to the other side of the bed, which was located in the middle of the room. I laid down behind Howard and kissed him on the cheek. No one said a word for what seemed to be about 15 minutes. The woman kept combing the little girl's hair, and Howard and I watched the television. The whole time, I'm thinking, "They are up here watching my television, laying on the bed I bought and eating the food I probably bought that was in the small refrigerator I had given Howard, when I moved out of my dorm room on campus.

So finally I asked Howard, "Who is this woman? He answered, "She is just a friend." At this response, the woman sent the little girl down stairs and stood up. She looked at Howard and said, "So, I'm just a friend?" This question was just the beginning of the floodgate of statements and questions she began to spew out of her mouth. She continued to say, "If we are just friends, then why are the majority of your clothes at my house?" If we are just friends, then why are you at my house every night after you get off the phone with her (meaning me) at 11:00 P.M.?" I knew she had to be telling the truth, because Howard and I had decided to get off the phone with each other at 11:00 P.M. every night so as to not run up charges for long distance calls. I looked at her and told her that I had heard enough from her. I began to spew my own facts, while waving my one carat marque diamond ring in her face. I asked, "Did he not tell you that he was engaged to be marry? Did he not tell you that he had a finance?" She replied, "He told me he had a girlfriend, but nothing about being engaged." I said, "Well he is engaged. You did not even care if he had a girlfriend, obviously." We went back and forth for a few minutes, then I glanced over at Howard and told him that he needed to make a decision with whom he wanted to be with. He told me that he wanted to be with me, of course. I told him, "Then you needed to make her leave." As he proceeded to tell her to leave, she said that she was not going anywhere. Here lies another one of my most embarrassing moments in this wrong relationship.

We all argued into the early morning. I do not even remember falling asleep; however, when I woke up, Howard, the other woman and I were all sitting or lying on his bed. I was so disgusted with myself. I heard Howard's mother hollering for him up the stairs. Howard's grandmother must have called her and told her what was going on. Howard went downstairs, and I could hear his mother tell him to get the other woman and her child out of the house. She told him that he should be ashamed of himself and should have never had both of us over at her mother's house arguing all night. The other woman went downstairs to leave, and Howard came back upstairs to talk with me. With tears running down my face, I got up and called my father, which I had never done in any of my relationships. I asked him to come over to Howard's house, so that I could get all my stuff: refrigerator, TV and other belongings. Howard, turned to me and said, "Why did you have to call your dad?" I told him that I was tired of the mess that he had put me through, and if he wanted to be with someone else, then he could have her.

Howard began to apologize and tell me that he loved me and wanted to be with me and that she did not mean anything to him. These were things I had heard so many times before; however, never did I have to compete with another woman in the relationship. I continued packing my things. I could tell Howard was furious that I had called my dad to come over and help me get my things from Howard's house. When my dad arrived, Howard helped me take my things to his car. What an oxymoron, my original abuser coming to rescue me from the one I thought was my savior, who turned out to be just like my dad. My dad asked me if he needed to do anything else, and I told him I was fine, and I would meet him at the house to help unload my stuff. As I got into the car, Howard went into the house, no longer speaking to me because I had called my dad.

As I drove off, I was crying uncontrollably. I could not believe Howard had been with someone else. All the abuse came rushing to my memory. The thoughts of, how I was doing everything to try to please Howard, yet he still decided to get involved with another woman. I had never experienced being number two in a relationship. I felt worthless. All the driving back and forth from Knoxville to Chattanooga. Waiting on Howard to get out of prison. Taking trips to Nashville to visit him, while he was in prison. Putting up with all the fights and jealousy was all for naught. When I got home, I remember seeing my stuff in the den where my dad put it. I went to my room and cried the rest of the weekend.

I went back to college and I was determined to finish my bachelor's degree with a decent grade point average, in spite of my current relationship with Howard on the brink of being over. He did call to apologize and tell me again that he loved me and wanted to be with me. However, I was not convinced down in my gut. But I went along with his sentiments, trying to believe in my heart that he would end the relationship with the other woman and marry me. I continued to be with Howard off and on for the last couple of months of my college season. I convinced myself that things would be different once I was at home and Howard and I were married. Everything would return back to normal and we would live happily ever after.

How many women of today can identify with this story? Yet, we stay in the wrong relationship way too long, and the only person that is completely deluded and stripped of all self-esteem, dignity, and value is the woman. The pressures of trying to hold onto the wrong relationship is emotionally and physically draining. But somehow women create this facade that they can change a man. This is so far from the truth. We convince ourselves that we cannot let go because we have invested so much time and energy into the relationship; that we would be foolish to let go now. If we end the relationship, who is going to want to be with us? We were never created for such drama and nonsense. The heart of a woman is delicate and fragile and only a true king knows how to appreciate the diamond that God has created.

PRAYER

Father, I pray that you will give my sister the strength and will to let go of all bad or wrong relationships. I pray that she will no longer deceive herself, thinking that he will change or that she can change him. I pray that she will allow you to change her from the inside out. I pray that you will restore dignity, self-esteem, worth and value back to her. I pray all the enemy's schemes and devices are destroyed off of her life. I pray every generational curse of abusive relationships be broken off her life today. I plead the blood of Jesus over her mind and heart. I pray that my sister will know how beautiful she is in your sight. Many are the compliments that you have toward her every day. I pray that my sister will be willing to give up the plans that she has created to be in position to receive all the great and mighty things that you have prepared for her before the foundation of the world. I pray that you will increase her faith and trust in you, Lord. Holy Spirit, comfort her heart and let her know the pain and suffering she is feeling right now, will pass with time and truth. Let her know that you have designed her destiny full of goodness and mercy all the days of her life.

EMPOWERMENT CONFESSIONS

We humans keep brainstorming options and plans,
but God's purpose prevails.
Proverbs 19:21 MSG

For we are His workmanship, created in Christ Jesus for good works,
which God prepared beforehand so that we would walk in them.
Ephesians 2:10

How precious also are Your thoughts to me, O God!
How vast is the sum of them!
If I should count them, they would outnumber the sand.
When I awake, I am still with You.
Psalms 139:17-18

Trust in the Lord with all your heart
And do not lean on your own understanding.
In all your ways acknowledge Him
and He will make your paths straight.
Proverbs 3:5-6

PART TWO: THE PRESSURE
THE NIGHT IN THE PARK

"You must make a decision that you are going to move on. It won't happen automatically. You will have to rise up and say, 'I don't care how hard this is, I don't care how disappointed I am, I'm not going to let this get the best of me. I'm moving on with my life."
— Joel Osteen

With only a few days until graduation, I was excited as well as confused about my relationship with Howard. We were still making plans to get married after graduation, but our relationship was definitely different. I really did not know if he had completely stopped seeing the other woman, Tonya. I discovered that Tonya was a girl he met at the hospital cafeteria where she worked. She had two children and was not interested in having any more kids. She had never been to college, and she lived in low-income housing. For the life of me, I could not figure out why Howard would choose her over me. I was about to be a college graduate, start an awesome career in finances, had no children and came from a working, middle-class family. In my eyes, I was totally the better choice for marriage material when you looked at both lifestyles. But, I was not the one who was doing the choosing.

I was growing closer to God during the last few months of college. I was reading my Bible and praying to God for answers about my relationship with Howard. Nonetheless, I was not completely sold out to God. I was still fornicating with Howard, which I justified since we were going to be married anyway. I was emotionally drained with trying to please Howard all the time. I mean I practically ate, breathed, and slept thinking about how I could make Howard happy. I was tired of being tired with all his jealousy, rules and complaints of what I was and was not doing for him. I found myself crying a lot, trying to keep our relationship together.

One night, I drove to the park to think and pray to God. I remember putting the sun roof back and looking up at the stars. Howard and I had just had a huge argument, again. I did not know what else I could do. I was doing everything in my power to make things work between us. As I cried uncontrollably, I remember asking God to fix our relationship, just fix it. I prayed, "God you can do anything that you want to do, so fix our relationship; make it better." I did not know how I had let things get so bad, but I was willing to stick it out, if God would intervene and fix the things in our relationship that were obviously broken. I stayed in the park for about two hours, just praying and crying. Once I felt peace, I drove back to my apartment near campus. The next few months would turn my world upside down. When you have been chosen by God to be a rare jewel, he will bring the diamond out of you. When you ask him to intervene, it is never how you expect.

After graduation, I decided to treat Howard and myself on a weekend trip to Gatlinburg. All expenses paid by me, of course. I wanted to show Howard that I was back in Chattanooga to stay, and I was willing to do anything to make our relationship work. This trip would be a fresh start for us. I thought we would rekindle our love for one another and forgive and forget the past. We arrived at the chalet and the first thing we saw when we checked into the cabin was a huge spider on the shower wall. I should have taken this as a sign that things would turn out for the worst. I had brought all the necessary items to the chalet to make our weekend as romantic as I could. From wine, candles and lingerie, to steaks and baked potatoes, I spared no expense, such as I could on a college graduate budget. We talked, laughed, and had sex the whole weekend. We did not talk about the other woman much at all. I wanted him to be totally focused on me and what I had given him all these years: my loyalty, friendship and love. I thought the weekend went exceptionally well, but during the drive home things changed drastically.

Howard became very distant and quiet as we drove down the expressway back home. When we arrived back in Chattanooga, I just knew that we would both go over to his house, like we used to. Howbeit, Howard told me to drop him off at his house, and he would call me later. I was devastated that he would treat me like a woman that he had just meet to have sex with and then throw away. It took all the strength that I had not to cry in front of him in that car, but I was not going to give him the pleasure of seeing my heart torn. He did not care that I had just spent all my money on food, wine and a chalet in Gatlinburg. He did not care that I had given my body, mind and soul to him over and over again. He never had any intentions of being with me. He just used me for a free weekend trip. He never called, so I called him, of course. And to no avail, he did not answer the phone. I felt degraded and misused again. I did not know how low I could allow a man to take me, but Howard literally took me to the hog pen. After the weekend trip, several days went by, and Howard would not accept my phone calls nor would he call me. So I began to spy on him, and I found out that he was still seeing Tonya. One day, I showed up at his house unannounced, and he completely disgraced me. Of course, the other woman was at the house with her children, and they were having a picnic. I was so hurt. He told me that I had no business showing up at his house without being invited and that he no longer wanted to see me or be with me. He also said that if I did not leave him and her alone that he would kill me. He dragged me out of his house in front of his family, Tonya and her kids. I was so embarrassed and humiliated. I cried all the way to my mother's house. I never included my mother or my dad in my relationship with Howard when we had problems. But this time, I did not know whom to turn to. I remember crying and trying to explain to my mom what had just transpired with Howard and me. I finally laid my head in my mother's lap. As she began to rub my head, she informed me that Howard was just like my dad. All the abuse, neglect, and having other women came rushing to my mind. I had fallen in lust, not love with someone just like my dad. What a horrible state to be in, which led me to want to end it all.

I could not believe Howard had decided to be with someone else. I did not have anyone to turn to who could speak life to me. I was at my lowest point. So one night, I decided I would commit suicide. I no longer wanted to live, if I could not be with Howard. I began to think about how I could end my life. I could take prescription drugs and fall asleep, but I did not have any. I hated to take medicine, anyway. I surely could not shoot myself, because I thought, "What if it did not work, and I lived through the gunshot?" So, I decided to drive off the Market Street Bridge.

As I was driving to the bridge, I was crying insuppressibly. I could no longer see the rode in front of me, so I pulled over to a side road to try to get myself together. I was seating in the car crying so much that the windows were fogged up, and I was beating the steering wheel asking the Lord, "Why he didn't fix my relationship." I was extremely disappointed and hurt by the way things had turned out. It was not supposed to end like this. What happened to me getting married and having two children by age 25? What happen to my rescuer? How did my life end up like this? All my life and time wasted and depleted. I had been with Howard for seven of my 21 years on this earth. Practically, all my young adult life. So if he did not want me, who would? All these thoughts rushed through my mind and soul. I was done, finished with being used and abused. Today, it would be all over, if I could only stop crying long enough to get to the bridge. Then I heard a knock on my window that startled me. The windows were so foggy that I had to let the window down to see who it might be. Who knew I was on this side road?

As I let the window down, I remember a man asking if everything was ok. "Did I need any help?" Looking away, I told the gentleman I was fine; however, anyone with any common sense could see that I was not fine. The gentleman then began to speak life to me. He told me "He is not worth it... God has a plan for your life. And it does not end like this." I turned in astonishment, to get a better look at the gentleman's face. However, I could not make out the gentlemen's face, due to the way the street light was shining behind his head. The light just shone around the gentleman's head, sort of like an aurora or halo. He went on to say, "You have so much to live for. You just don't realize it right now, but in due season, you will see. So stop crying, things will get better..." I bent my head downward towards my lap and when I raised my head to tell the gentleman thank you for stopping, he was gone. I collected myself and wiped my face. I turned on the defrost in the car, so I could see and began to drive home. I no longer wanted to end my life after this encounter. Looking back, I know this man was an angel sent by God to save me from my own detriment.

However, something did die that night and that was my relationship with Howard. It was officially and completely over. God did answer my prayer to fix the relationship. It was just not like I thought it would be fixed. I imagined Howard and I would be together, but

God saw differently. He ended it. And what happens when something dies? Here comes the process: grieving.

PRAYER

My sister, if you are reading this prayer, and you have experienced similar issues, then know you are a survivor! You have chosen to live and not die. Now I pray the Lord will heal your heart, your mind and soul. I pray the Lord will become the lover of your soul and you will no longer be entangled and weighed down with sin. I pray the Lord will silence every negative thought of confusion, disbelief and disappointment. I pray the Holy Spirit will fill you mind with thoughts of love and completeness in Christ Jesus. I pray against the spirit of suicide and death. You shall live and live life more abundantly. No more soul ties. I pray the Lord will break every emotional, physical and mental soul tie from past relationships off of your life. If you do not know Jesus as your personal Savior, then today is the day you can accept Him into your life. Pray this, "Father I confess all my wrong doings, all my sins. I realize that I need you to take over my life and make me new. Father, I repent. Restore me to my original design and purpose that you created for me. I receive all that you have given me and I welcome the Holy Spirit to consume me and teach me how to live on purpose. I thank you for saving me."

If you prayed this prayer, then you are now a new creature in Christ Jesus; old things are passing away and behold all things are becoming new. My sister, you are made new, but remember it is a process of giving up your old nature, and allowing Jesus to be Lord of your life. God's purpose and plans shall prevail. I pray that his Word will keep you.

EMPOWERMENT CONFESSIONS

I shall not die, but live, and declare the works of the Lord.
Psalm 118:17

The thief comes only to steal and kill and destroy; I came that they
may have life, and have it abundantly.
John 10:10

For you have died and your life is hidden with Christ in God.
When Christ, who is our life…
Colossians 3:3-4

You've already put in your time in that God-ignorant way of life,
partying night after night, a drunken and profligate life. Now it's
time to be done with it for good. Of course, your old friends don't
understand why you don't join in with the old gang anymore. But
you don't have to give an account to them. They're the ones who
will be called on the carpet—and before God himself.
I Peter 4:3-5 MSG

We are destroying speculations and every lofty thing raised up
against the knowledge of God, and we are taking every thought
captive to the obedience of Christ.
2 Corinthians 10:5

Therefore if anyone is in Christ, he is a new creature; the old things
passed away; behold, new things have come.
2 Corinthians 5:17

That if you confess with your mouth Jesus as Lord, and believe in
your heart that God raised Him from the dead, you will be saved; for
with the heart a person believes, resulting in righteousness, and with
the mouth he confesses, resulting in salvation. - Romans 10:9-10

PART THREE: THE PROCESS
KNOW THE TRUTH – DON'T FALL FOR THE COUNTERFEIT

True glory takes root, and even spreads; all false pretences, like flowers, fall to the ground; nor can any counterfeit last long.
- Marcus Tullius Cicero

My life became a routine, so I could keep myself sane from the breakup with Howard. I realized I had made him my god. I was so consumed with trying to make him happy that my true God, removed him from my life completely. This was the season of my life that I began to draw even closer to the Lord. My life consisted of work, exercising at the gym and studying the Word of God. My older sister would try to set me up with men for dates and to hang out with, but I did not want to have anything to do with men. My prayer to God was "do not make me bitter towards men, so as not to miss my husband when he does come along. However, I do not want another man to even approach me unless he is the one."

One night, my sister called me to inform me something had happened to our mother. She was in jail for some reason. I did not know if it was drug related or if something seriously had happened to her. So my older sister and I went down to the city jail to see what we needed to do to bail her out. I did not know anything about getting someone out of jail, but my sister knew that we needed a bail bondsman. We ended up getting in contact with a bail bondsman company that was owned by a gentleman named Harrison.

Harrison pulled up beside us as we sat outside the downtown jail. I was sitting in the driver's seat when he rolled down his window and introduced himself. He informed us how much we needed to pay him to get my mother out of jail. He had a pretty smile; however, he was light-skinned, like a "light bright." My sister nudged me in the arm and said, "He is nice looking." You should give him your phone number." I turned to her and said, "You know I'm not looking for a man." She said, "So what, you could lighten up and have some fun." Well, he overheard our conversation and laughed. My sister started asking him questions like, "Are you married? Are you dating anyone?" He told her he was divorced and not dating anyone at the time. She asked how old he was, and reluctantly he told her 35 years old. I looked at her and rolled my eyes. I directed the conversation back to getting my mom out of jail. Harrison stated the cost and I handed him the money. He instructed us to wait outside while he went in to retrieve our mom. I did not know that we would be waiting a long time before our mom was released. Inevitably, the conversation with Harrison lasted longer than I desired. He came back out and told us that it would be about an hour before our mom would be released. My sister went back into matchmaker mode, asking more personal questions. She told him that I had recently graduated from college with a bachelor's in Finance and Accounting. She proceeded to tell him I was single as well. I gave her the evil eye and told her to stop telling all my business. Since she refused to stop, I began to ask Harrison some questions of my own. I asked Harrison if he was saved. Did he have a personal relationship with the Lord?

He told us that he was a believer and that he had been walking with the Lord for a while. He informed us that he attended a church called New United. He invited us to attend sometime. He also told us he believed that the Lord had told him to go back to his wife. I thought it was great that he knew what the Lord was leading and guiding him to do in his life. After about an hour had gone by, we learned that Harrison was very charming, easy to talk to, and very loyal to his family. He owned several businesses and loved to travel. I turned my eyes toward my mom as I saw her emerge from the government building, holding her head down in shame. I thanked Harrison for all his help. My sister blurted out my phone number to him and told him to call me. My mom slid into the car and we drove off.

A few weeks had gone by, and Harrison called and invited me to go to his church. I decided this was harmless, especially since I was looking for a good church to attend, so I said "yes." I wanted to make sure Harrison knew I was definitely not interested in dating, so I invited my sister and mom to attend church with me. After Sunday service, he invited my family and me out to dinner, his treat. Of course, the family said "yes" before I could even respond. Harrison hit it off with my mom and sister at dinner, and we had a great time talking about the sermon the pastor had preached and getting to know one another. After we departed from dinner, I went home to study. Harrison called later and told me that he had a great time with me and my family. I let him know I enjoyed visiting his church. I really learned a lot and would probably visit again. Harrison asked if he could see me again and I told him, yes I would see him at church next Sunday.

After a few more visits to the church, I joined New United. I was excited about the teaching I was getting from the pastor and in my own personal study time with the Lord. The choir at the church was "off the chain" as well. I really loved the worship time at church. It helped me to get over Howard. I would cry almost every time I was in worship at church. I thought my tear ducts where going to dry up from all the crying I was doing about the breakup with Howard. I would cry out to the Lord, asking him, "Am I ever going to get over the relationship I had with Howard?" Only time, prayer and the word of God would mend my heart from the seven years I spent with Howard. I wanted the pain to go away immediately.

Indeed, Harrison continued to pursue me, but it was very subtlety. He would invite me to dinner after church every Sunday. Then he would drop by my job unexpectantly and take me to lunch. It was nice having someone to talk to about anything. Harrison was a great conversationalist. We could talk about anything, from sports and politics to business and the Bible. Harrison was very well versed with the scriptures, and we often talked for hours about the word of God. I was beginning to really like Harrison, and he felt the same way about me. It seemed like overnight our relationship was changing from just being friends to something more.

Harrison spared no expense when we were together. We would take spontaneous trips to Atlanta to see a Brave's game or just to shop. Harrison was like a breath of fresh air from all the abuse and pain I experienced with Howard. My family loved Harrison as well. And they were all for us being together as a couple. Harrison was so careful with me. He was not harsh or brute in any way. He really treated me like a queen. I attributed his mannerisms with me to his relationship with the Lord and our age difference. He was 13 years older than I. I often thought about the age difference between us, but Harrison never brought it up. I began to spend time with Harrison every day. We began to share intimate and personal history with each other. There was nothing that Harrison would not do for me. Harrison was in my life when my mom got delivered from drugs. This was a very happy time in my life. I started to believe that Harrison was my husband, and I was falling for him hard.

Harrison would tell me that he loved me and wine and dine me all the time. However, he never changed his confession of believing that the Lord had told him that he was supposed to reconcile with his wife. I tried to convince myself that it did not matter what Harrison believed; I was here now with him. His wife was in Alabama somewhere. Again, I thought I could change the way Harrison believed. Our relationship became more intimate as well. I started to sleep with Harrison. However, both of us felt much conviction afterwards. We knew this was not pleasing to the Lord. We tried to stop seeing each other; unfortunately, we had gotten so comfortable with the relationship and being together every day. Then the torture began. I would ask Harrison, "When do you plan on marrying me?" He would evade the question, by telling me he loved me and then take me out somewhere extravagant or buy me an expensive gift.

I had been dating Harrison for about nine months before I came to my senses. I finally came to the conclusion I was still playing second best in a man's life. Even though, I had given Harrison every part of me, he still wanted to go back to his wife. Foolishly, I was competing against another woman in a relationship when I deserved to be number one. No matter how wonderfully, Harrison treated me, he did not want to make me his wife. And that is what I wanted to be: a wife, not a side chick. Again, I had given my heart to someone, only for him to trample over it. Harrison was the counterfeit. Even though he was nice and not abusive, he still wanted me to be his women in Chattanooga, but cling to the hopes of being reconciled with his ex-wife.

In early October, I made a decision that I was done with the relationship with Harrison. I called him and told him that I loved him; however, I realized that he did not want to marry me. He was sentimental and courteous by telling me I was going to make some man very happy and be a good wife. He loved me, but he had to obey the Lord. He still wanted to see me, but I had to obey the Lord as well and get out of the relationship. It was really hard not to talk with him. He would call every day; I ignored his phone calls. I needed to get as far away from him as I could. And that meant cutting all soul ties with him. I remember the enemy telling me, "Why would you break up with Harrison a month before your birthday. You are not going to be able to go out to dinner. You are not going to get any birthday gifts." I made a decision that my heart was more important than just having someone to be with during special occasions like birthdays, Christmas or Thanksgiving. I had to learn to value and love myself, while truly being single. So I turned my heart, mind and soul to the truth, Jesus Christ.

I will never forget the time God showed me real love. I was praying the morning of my birthday. Just thanking the Lord for allowing me to see another year. I am not one who likes surprise birthdays or people to make a big deal about my birthday. But I remember praying and thinking that it would sure be nice to have a small, intimate birthday party, and I would like to receive some flowers for my birthday. I shared this request with no one, but God. I continued on with my usual routine; work and then exercise. Later on in the evening, I had to attend one of my Bible study classes at church. The teacher decided to break the monotony and have the class at her house. Well, much to my surprise, when I arrived at the teacher's house and walked through the door, all my classmates yelled, "Surprise! Happy Birthday!" The entire room was decorated with balloons and candles. And then one of my classmates brought out a vase full of beautiful red and white roses as a gift to me from the class. I nearly fell to my knees in astonishment and unbelief. I began to cry uncontrollably. Everyone was trying to figure out what was the matter with me, but I was so overwhelmed with joy. All I kept saying was that the Lord really loves me.

So many times, we as women believe in order to be showed true love, it has to come from the person we are dating or the opposite sex. We have been so deceived by the world, society and other people that true love has to come from a man, not so. We have been tricked to believe that the only way gifts and flowers can really mean something is if a man gives them to us. But God showed me differently and he can do the same for you. The Lord knows how to show you real love with no strings attached. Because he is love, that's a noun, not a verb. You cannot recognize the love of the Father, if you have an imposter in His place.

I believe when you are truly seeking the will of the Lord, the enemy will try to seduce you with a counterfeit. It may look like God, smell like God, and even act like God. But as a true woman of God, you must not ignore the signs the Lord is giving you to make you aware of what is counterfeit and what is true. From the very beginning of my conversation with Harrison, the Lord revealed to me that he was supposed to go back to his wife. However, I ignored this bit of information and got sucked into another emotional soul tie. I know now that Harrison was to lead me to New United, the church, where I would spend a season learning to be single for the Lord, and that was it.

PRAYER

Lord, I pray that my sister will know the truth and the truth shall make her free. I pray that she will recognize counterfeit when it comes in her direction. I pray that she will take the way of escape. I pray that she will not be weak and desperate to be in another relationship, where a man will not make her number one. I pray that she is coming into her true value and worth. Let the Lord, Jesus Christ be the lover of your soul. God is not ignorant of your desire to be a wife. He has created someone just for you. I pray that any man who comes along in your life and shows interest, that you will follow the truth, the Word of God. The Holy Spirit will lead and guide you into all truth. Be patient, my sister, and wait on the Lord. It pleases the Father to bless you with good things.

EMPOWERMENT CONFESSIONS

"If you continue in My word, then you are truly disciples of Mine; you will know the truth, and the truth will make you free." So if the Son makes you free, you will be free indeed.
John 8:31-32, 36

Sanctify them in the truth; Your word is truth.
John 17:17

No temptation has overtaken you but such as is common to man; and God is faithful, who will not allow you to be tempted beyond what you are able, but with the temptation will provide the way of escape also, so that you will be able to endure it.
I Corinthians 10:13

For men will be....treacherous, reckless, conceited, lovers of pleasure rather than lovers of God, holding to a form of godliness, although they have denied its power; Avoid such men as these. For among them are those who enter into households and captivate weak women weighed down with sins, led on by various impulses, always learning and never able to come to the knowledge of the truth.
2 Timothy 3:4-7

And He said to him, "You shall love the Lord your God with all your heart, and with all your soul, and with all your mind."
Matthew 22:37

Yet those who [a]wait for the Lord
Will gain new strength;
They will mount up with wings like eagles,
They will run and not get tired,
They will walk and not become weary.
Isaiah 40:31

If you then, being evil, know how to give good gifts to your children, how much more will your Father who is in heaven give what is good to those who ask Him!
Matthew 7:11

PART THREE: THE PROCESS
BEING SINGLE, BUT NOT ALONE

I don't need a man to rectify my existence. The most profound relationship we'll ever have is the one with ourselves."
--Shirley MacLaine

"A productive, vibrant, goal-oriented woman is so much more attractive than a woman who waits around for a man to validate her existence." --Mandy Hale

Single, only one, absent from another person or thing. I had never experienced this season before in my adulthood. Single, solidarity, unique, oneness. I was ready to live as the Word of God stated a single person should live. I Corinthians 7:32 says, "One who is unmarried is concerned about the things of the Lord, how he may please the Lord." I was back to my routine life and I was determined to please the Lord and allow Him to truly be Lord of all of me. I still desired to be married, but I wanted the Lord to prepare me to be the wife to the husband who he had for me. I no longer wanted to choose. No more dating, no more male conversations, no more friends just to talk to or go out on dates with. To some it may have seemed as if I was alone, but I was not. I began a beautiful journey of the self-discovery of me.

I became heavily involved in the church, New United. Taking every small group Bible study, I could attend. I needed to figure out what truly made me happy in a relationship. Better yet, I needed to find out who I really was. For the majority of my life, I had been engrossed in being any and everything to try to please my father, Howard and Harrison that I did not really know who I was.

For my earthly father, I tried to be the proud daughter that he claimed to have sent through college. But this was far from the truth. He did help pack my stuff up in his van and transported me to college, but by no means did he pay for me to go through college. The student loans I paid back is what supported me while I was in college. So there was no reason to feel obligated to trying to please him anymore. I had to learn to forgive my parents, especially my father. He had this famous saying when I was growing up that he would tell my siblings and me. He would say, "I did the best that I could." Meaning that he did the best that he could do with taking care of us or providing for us. However, as I learned through the word of God that a good father leaves an inheritance for his children's children (grandchildren), I realized that this statement was no longer true nor valid enough for me to continue to listen to it be spoken.

Remember, my father was very abusive, so it took the Holy Spirit breathing through me to confront my father about the way he had treated me in my childhood. This was just a part of the process that I had to go through to appreciate my earthly DNA, which ultimately helped me to appreciate myself. One day, my father came home; I was studying in my bedroom. Normally, he headed straight to his bedroom, but this time he stopped and knocked on my bedroom door. I acknowledged the knock and told him to come in. He opened my bedroom door and asked me what I was doing. I told him I was studying and praying, and the Lord had revealed to me that I could not attend his deacon ordination. See, my father had always wanted to become a deacon. I believe this was a goal of his, to complete some social status quo. However, I knew, according to the word of God, his character and lifestyle did not line up with the description of being a deacon. He still had several women, and to top it all off, he had just gotten married to the pastor's daughter the previous weekend. Plus, I knew he was still dating a woman that he had been with for over seven years. I asked him if he wanted to know why I was not going to attend the ordination, and he said no. I proceeded to tell him that I forgave him for all the abuse he posed upon me, my mom and siblings. My father used to have a statement that he would make all the time, when it came to explaining how he raised us. He would say, I did the best that I could" I told him that this statement was a lie. I said, "The best that you could have done was come home at night to your wife and children." Instead you decided to be with other women and their children." Even if he was going to be with other women, he could have at least come home at night and kept us when my mother had to work third shift to make ends meet for our family. I told him I would pray that God would make him all the man that he desired to be. I forgave him and told him that I was learning to love him as Christ does. My father was very quiet as tears ran down his face. I had never seen my father cry before.

Nonetheless, this conversation freed me completely from trying to please him in anyway except as God would have me to. No more feeling obligated or fearful of him, just pure love. I began to pray for my dad as I would a brother in Christ. Realizing that he too, was created by God, in spite of his past or his present state.

As for Howard, it would take a long time to get him out of my system. I wondered what I ever did to him, for him to choose someone else. Howard and I had not spoken for over a year, but I still visited his grandmother from time to time. Ms. Joy was like my grandmother, so I would still buy her cigarettes and take them to her house, when I went to check up on how she was doing. As I went by the house one time, something was different. I entered the house and gave Ms. Joy a hug. I always asked how our "boy" was doing; "boy" meaning Howard. Deep down inside of me, I think a part of me wanted Howard to walk through the door while I visited his grandmother. I just wanted to see his face, hear his voice, and see his smile. She answered and said he was doing fine. As I turned to sit down on the couch, my eyes caught the pictures on the fire place mantle. They were wedding pictures. Yes, Howard's wedding pictures to the other woman that he cheated on me with. I almost missed my seat on that couch and fell on the floor. It took everything in me not to cry. However, I did not want her to see me cry. I had cried enough over him. I asked, "When did Howard get married?" Ms. Joy said that he had just gotten married two weeks ago. My memory came rushing back to me of the date we had set to get married, and lo and behold, this was the exact date he had married the other woman on. And here I was sitting in his grandmother's house, and he was off on his honeymoon. Again I felt like running off a cliff somewhere and ending my life. He could have picked any other day to get marry on, but no. This was one more thing to hurt me. Then I heard the Holy Spirit say to me, "You keep hurting yourself, every time you go visit Ms. Joy. She is not your family. The only thing that you have in common with her is her grandson. If it was not for him, you would not even know her." At that point I collected myself, told Ms. Joy goodbye and I left her house. When I got in my car, of course, I could no longer contain the tears, so the floodgates opened up. I cried all the way home. But I made an important decision that day. I would never visit his grandmother again. I had to stop putting myself in positions to be hurt. If I wanted to completely heal from my relationship with Howard, I had to let everything that was attached to him exit out of my life. I was no longer going to walk in bondage of what could have been. I had to learn that I was enough, just the way that the Lord created me. I had to learn to love me, in spite of my past.

Women of the 21st century tend to stay in relationship with the family and friends of past relationships. We are afraid to cut away everything that is tied to the man who hurt us, including their family and friends. But we do not recognize that this is the very thing that keeps us in bondage to the man we swear we have let go. You are only deceiving yourself, if you truly believe this lie. We must be willing to release everything and everyone associated with the man.

In order to obtain complete healing, you must make a conscience decision to let go and let God.

My season of singleness taught me I was deserving of a wonderful husband. I learned through the word of God, that I was valuable and created to succeed. I learned that I did not need a man to complete me, but that I was complete in Christ. I learned as a single woman, how to carry myself, in speech and conduct. I learned that I could not go everywhere and be in association with everyone. I was on a journey of loving me, forgiving the people who had hurt me, and embracing my walk with the Lord.

I loved to study the word of God. I became very protective of what I allowed to enter my eye gate and my ear gate. Which meant, I did not listen to R&B music any more. Why you ask? Because it brought back too many memories of my childhood and past relationships. I stopped watching TV except on Thursday nights, when I would watch the Cosby show. Watching love stories or movies just made me want to be in a relationship, so TV had to go. While taking Bible classes at the church and studying on my own, I learned I was gifted in teaching, prophecy, discernment and administration. So, I began to teach some of the small group Bible classes at church as well. Some may say, well your life became very boring or strict. On the contrary, it was not. The Lord was revealing to me every day who I was, what he created me to do and where I was going. Previously, I had been so focused on being married and in a relationship that I did not even know the gifts and callings that I possessed to impact the world. When you are so consumed with pleasing someone else, then you are operating in idolatry. You do not have to be worshipping a golden calf or statue to practice idolatry. Anything you put in the place of God is idolatry, and the Lord will have none of that if you truly belong to Him. Yes, being single is great, but you are never alone. The Lord was with me every step of the way. And He will be with you as well, my jewel.

PRAYER

Lord, I pray as my sister embarks upon unchartered territory, that she will know that she is not alone. I pray that you will realize that being single is not a curse or a fad. But it is a time to truly find out who you are and what you deserve. I pray strength and peace as you forgive family, friends and enemies that have despitefully hurt you. I pray that you will learn to love yourself, which in turn will allow you to love others, without looking for something in return. I pray that you will know that you are complete in Christ, all one. You do not need a man to complete you. I pray that you will embrace the gifts and callings that the Lord has placed inside of you. I pray that you realize that you were to be more than a wife. God has great and mighty things for you to do. Seek the Lord with all your heart, with all your soul and with all your mind. You have been bought with a price, you are not your own. Your body belongs to the Lord, so be mindful that you embody the Holy Spirit. I pray that you will enjoy your season of singleness, knowing that a single person cares about how they can please the Lord. I pray that you will have a hunger and thirst for the word of God and your joy will be complete in Him.

EMPOWERMENT CONFESSIONS

We proclaim Him, admonishing every man and teaching every man with all wisdom, so that we may present every man complete in Christ.
Colossians 1:28

But if you do not forgive, neither will your Father who is in heaven forgive your transgressions.
Mark 11:26

Be kind to one another, tender-hearted, forgiving each other, just as God in Christ also has forgiven you.
Ephesians 4:32

He who loves father or mother more than Me is not worthy of Me.
Matthew 10:37

I will not fail you nor forsake you.
Joshua 1:5

Peace I leave with you; My peace I give to you; not as the world gives do I give to you. Do not let your heart be troubled, nor let it be fearful.
John 14:27

Since we have gifts that differ according to the grace given to us, each of us is to exercise them accordingly.
Romans 12:6

PART THREE: THE PROCESS
ONCE YOU OUT, STAY OUT

"Letting go means to come to the realization that some people are a part of your history, but not a part of your destiny."
— Steve Maraboli

Being what I call a book girl, I have learned that tests come along in your life to test your knowledge, love, faith, trust, character, integrity and belief in God. You should not treat your relationship with God as if he were Santa Claus, because God judges your heart. If you are going to live for God, it is an everyday choice to give up your will and follow His way in complete obedience. Just as a rare jewel must go through the fire to remove all impurities, so must our lives, to remove all residue from the past and to increase our faith. Who will you depend on in the time of need? Who will you turn to when you feel alone? What will you do when your flesh cries out for attention?

I had been living single for almost a year. I felt confident of who I was and whom I belonged to: God. I was working a fairly good job, focused on getting out of debt and going to graduate school. I was living at my dad's house, trying to save money and pay off student loans. A normal day for me during this season of my life was very predictable. I went to work, worked out and then studied the word of God. I attended church on Wednesday night for Bible study and on Sundays. I visited my mom every week and talked with my siblings occasionally. One day, I went to work out at the downtown gym, my usual place. Most of the men that worked out there every day knew me by name, but they called me the "stair master queen," because I would come into the gym with my headphones on and get right on the stair master for an hour. The men treated me like their little sister. If someone came into the gym and flirted with me or asked one of them who I was, they would immediately tell them, "She is waiting on her husband. She does not date." I had told so many of them that I didn't date, that they started telling anyone that was new to the gym the same thing, so guys did not even approach me in the gym. I liked this scenario. It allowed me to come work out in peace, without distractions or foolishness. However, this day was different.

I decided to start with the exercise bike and listen to some Joyce Meyers teaching tapes. Just as I was sitting down on the bike, I looked down to turn my headphones to play. As I looked back up, to my surprise, who do I see walk by in front of my bike: Howard. My eyes fixated upon him. It was like I entered into a trance. I could smell his cologne, see his biceps and triceps and that pretty smile. He looked fine! I always tell young ladies that I mentor today to know thyself. Meaning know your weaknesses and temptations. Now all this time I had been working out at the same gym for over a year and he had never come into this gym. Even though I had just arrived at the gym, not even 15 minutes into my workout. I got myself off that bike, grabbed my gym bag and left! The Bible tells us to flee from lusts and pursue righteousness and that is exactly what I did. I thought to myself, "If he even speaks to me, I am going to be in trouble." But know that the devil does not give up so quickly.

I arrived home, got ready to take a shower and my phone rang. Now, this was during the time when caller id boxes were connected separately to the phone. I usually screened my phone calls anyway, so I glanced at the caller id box to see who was calling me. The name on the box was a name that I recognized from my high school days. Johnathon was Howard's best friend in high school. Now I was trying to figure out how he got my phone number and why he was calling me. So, of course, I did not answer, and I let him leave a message on the phone. This was also during the time when you could hear a person leave you a voice message out loud. I heard Johnathan say, "Niscey, your boy left you a note outside on your car. He said get the note and give him a call." I knew exactly who he was referring to as "my boy," it was Howard. I ignored the message, and then the phone rang again. It was Johnathan leaving another message. This time he said, "Your boy asked will you please go get the note off the car. He knows that you are at home." I froze in place, thinking what I should do? I did not think that Howard even noticed me at the gym, but he must have. How did he know where I lived? How did he get my dad's phone number? I went outside, nervously looking around, since it was late at night. I did not know if Howard would be outside parked down the street watching me or something else crazy. I ran to the car and lo and behold there was a note under the windshield wiper. I grabbed the note and ran back into the house.

The note said, "Please call me. I need to talk with you." I was nervous and curious at the same time. I had not spoken to Howard in over a year. What could he possible say to me at this point that I would want to hear? I decided not to call him, but I guess he saw me retrieve the note off the car, and the next phone call was from him. I saw Howard's name show up on the caller id box, and so many memories came rushing to my mind. Everything in my mind said, "Do not answer that phone," but my heart spoke something different. Once I answered the phone and heard Howard's, deep voice asking, "What are you doing?" I paused before I answered and then I started asking questions, like "Why are you calling me? Where is your wife? How did you get my home phone number? How did you know where I lived? He answered my questions with one resounding comment, "Niscey, I have always known how to find you." He asked me why I left the gym when I saw him. I told him that I know the devil when I see it. He laughed and asked "Why do you call me the devil?" I informed him, that he was not the devil himself, but probably being used by the devil. We made small talk a few more minutes. I told him that I do not talk with married men. He ignored the statement and expressed how happy he was to see me at the gym. He really wished that I had not run off so quickly. He confessed that he never stopped loving me and that I could call him at any time if I ever needed something. With this remark, I got angry with Howard. I advised him that he could not do anything for me. He was married, and I was not playing second best again. I then proceeded to hang up the phone in his face. I was so furious with myself for having a conversation with him. He was still the same. He called back and apologized for making me upset. He just wanted me to know if I needed anything I could call him, no strings attached. I accepted his apology and hung up the phone.

Howard showing back up in my life brought about many mixed emotions. I found myself thinking about him at times, especially since I was having financial problems. Howard was always a good provider in our relationship. He was willing to give or buy me anything that I needed or wanted. At this point, I was trying to juggle student loans, car payment and daily expenses like food and gas. Some extra cash would certainly provide a little relief to my situation. I was very tempted to call him and ask for help.

Howard was very persistent in pursuing a new relationship with me. He began to call me every other day. Sometimes I would answer and other times I would not. We talked about his family, especially his grandmother, whom I was very close to. One day, he even asked to borrow my plunger to unclog a toilet. I felt like this was an excuse to see me, so I told him that I would leave the plunger outside on the porch, and he could pick it up from there. Since the plunger did not work, Howard asked if I would help him on an assignment that he had for his business. He was a licensed plumber. Of course, I told him no, at first. He proceeded to tell me that he would pay me $100 if I would just come and hold the flashlight while he fixed a pipe.

How could I turn down $100 that would be so easily given to me for practically doing nothing? Here I go again, falling for the person that hurt me so much, but not just for love, but for money this time. So, I agreed to meet Howard at the location that he instructed me to go to. The house was far out in the suburbs, so I was a little nervous at first. When I pulled around the corner, there was Howard, with his fine self, standing in the street in front of the house to greet me. I had not seen him since the time at the gym, even though we had been communicating on the phone with each other. His broad shoulders, handsome smile and tall stance put me in a trance for a moment as I gazed upon him. I quickly gathered myself together. Howard walked toward the car and I rolled down the window. He asked, "How are you going to hold the flashlight sitting in the car?" I laughed and got out of the car and followed him into the house. Nobody was home at this house that he had led me to. I made sure to ask if this was his house. He gave me a look and assured me that it was not his home. I did not want to be running into his wife. Howard was working on the kitchen sink, replacing some piping. I did as I was asked and held the flashlight. It took all of about 20 minutes for Howard to replace the piping. As we were walking out of the house together, he grabbed my hand. It startled me as first, but I did not pull away. As we got outside, we lingered in the street talking, laughing and enjoying one another's company. He kept holding my hand and pulling me close to him as we talked leaning against his car. It began to get dark outside. I told Howard that I needed to head toward home. He walked me to the car and gave me a $100 bill. He told me that he appreciated me coming to help him, and he would have paid any price to see me again. He leaned down and grabbed me around my waist and hugged me tight. My hands naturally went up around his neck, and my head was buried into his chest. It definitely felt like old times. I did not want him to let me go. Howard bent down to kiss me on my neck, and I pulled away. I told him, "Don't forget that you are married." When I said those words, it was as if I snapped myself back into reality. I quickly said my goodbyes and got in my car and drove away. I heard my pager going off; indeed it was him. I called him and he asked, why I left so abruptly? I told him that I did not need to be hanging out with him longer. He had a wife and kids to get home to. And I needed to get home as well. He asked when he could see me again, and I told him never. He told me that he never stopped loving me, and today reminded him of old times and of how much he missed being with me. I could not take hearing these words, so I told him that he had his chance to be with me, and he blew it. I hung up the phone in his face. I began to get angry at the fact that now he expresses that he wants to be with me and he misses me. That was a bunch of garbage, and I did not need to let myself get entangled with his lies or statements, because at the end of the day, he was still married.

A few days went by, and I tried to ignore Howard's phone calls and pages. I felt myself being torn with wanting to be with him and knowing that I could not. One night Howard called me at 2:00AM in the morning. I answered the phone by saying, "What does the devil want?" I heard his deep voice ask, "Why are you calling me the devil?" I told him that nobody calls someone at 2:00AM in the morning except the devil. He laughed. Howard ventured to tell me that he had put his wife out of the house. There was silence on the phone for what seemed like five minutes. Howard asked me, "Did you hear me?" I immediately told him that he was wrong. I began to quote scriptures to him, like someone shooting an Uzi. I told him as a husband he had no right to get rid of his wife. I told him that he needed to work things out with his wife. He needed to pray and call out to the Lord to save his marriage. I told him that he did not need to be talking to me, but his wife. When I finally calmed down from being Evangelist Niscey, he stated he only wanted someone to talk to about the fight that he had with his wife. At the sound of these words, it was if the Holy Spirit of injustice had descended upon me. I was infuriated with the fact that he thought that he could just call me to console him about his wife. I thought to myself, "Where was he when I needed to talk to someone to get over my relationship with him? Who did I have to turn to in the midnight hour, when I was crying and agonizing over him?" No one, but the Holy Spirit. My next words to Howard were spoken distinctly and with conviction. I told him he needed to fall on his knees, ask God for forgiveness for putting his wife out and call out to God to help him. I informed Howard not to call me anymore, because we no longer had anything else to discuss. He was married and that was final. I said good night sharply and slammed the phone down. I prayed to the Lord that night to help me to get Howard completely out of my system. I no longer wanted to feel anything for him. I confessed and repented for giving him any of my time over the last few months. I knew I had no business spending time with a married man. I needed help to resist him. Little, did I know that closure was closer than I thought.

I did not hear from Howard for several weeks. I was glad because my emotions were all over the place. I was thinking about why God allowed him to come back into my life. He was married to the woman that he decided to leave me for and a father to her children. I had been walking with the Lord circumspectively and faithfully. I did not need any distractions from my relationship with the Lord. But here he comes with all his suaveness and protective nature, which I adored and needed earlier in my life. During times of brokenness and despair, Howard had been my rescuer and provider. Now I know better, God is the only true savior and provider. My knowledge of knowing God would have to extend further than just head knowledge, but it would have to become the will and obedience of my heart.

I remember like it was yesterday; the last time I laid eyes upon Howard. It would prove to be a major turning point in my life. One Saturday afternoon, I was home cleaning the house and he called and asked if he could return my plunger that he had borrowed several months earlier. I was shocked to hear his voice, so upon his request I told him that it would be fine for him to return the plunger. I gave him a specific time that was during daylight hours. When he arrived, as usual, he looked and smelled nice. I met him on the porch, because I was a little apprehensive about inviting him into the house. He gave me the plunger and then asked if I was going to invite him into the house. I asked him, "Why do you need to come in my house?" He told me he wanted to sit down and tell me something. He had this serious look on his face, so I yielded to his request and he followed me into the house. I motioned for him to sit on the couch. As he sat, I walked over to sit in the chair. He asked me why I did not want to sit next to him on the couch. I told him I was fine in the chair, and there was no need for us to be sitting so close together. He laughed. I did not want to have him in the house for very long, so I quickly asked him, "What do you need to tell me?" He tried to make small talk by asking me if I would turn the television on. I informed him that I did not watch TV, besides on Thursday evenings when the *Cosby's* and *Living Single* aired during the week. Again I spoke with directness, "What did you need to tell me?" He sat up on the couch and said the words that I had been wanting to hear since the day I caught him upstairs in the bed with the other woman. He started by rephrasing the question I would ask him over and over again when he was dragging my heart through the mud. He responded, "You know that question you would ask me, about what you did to make me leave you? Well, you did nothing. I was the one that was impatient. You were the best thing that ever happened to me. And I messed it up. I want to apologize for all the hurt that I put you through. And I ask you to please forgive me?" When my ears and heart heard those words, it was as if the Holy Spirit said, "It is finished." I told Howard I had forgiven him a long time ago. In order for me not to be bitter or just a "mad black woman," I had to forgive him. I had to forgive him, so that the Lord could prepare me to be the wife He needed me to be to the husband that He had created for me.

I advised Howard that it was time for him to leave after he had expressed his apologies. He looked at me with confusion. I told him that there was no need for him to stay any longer. He got up without any further hesitation. I stood on the porch as he walked toward his car in front of the house. He walked back towards me and stood at the bottom of the stairs, which made him and me the same height, face to face, eye to eye. He repeated words that I had heard him say several times, "I love you, and we are always going to be together, no matter what." And then he leaned in to kiss me. I quickly moved back and said these famous Ebonics words, "Don't do me!" I explained to him that if it was meant for us to be together, then he would have never married the other woman. If it was meant for us to be together, then no matter how many fights, disagreements or trials that we may have faced, we would be together right now. And this was not the case. I expressed to him that God had something better in store for me and it was not playing second to his wife. I told him goodbye for the final time and walked into the house. I watched him as he got into the car and drove away, never to darken my life again. I felt relieved, exuberant, refreshed and alive. It was finally over, and I am alive to tell someone else that if God did it for me, He will do it for you. I passed the test and I am more in love with God than ever before. He is truly the lover of my soul. I truly know what it means to care about the things of the Lord as a single woman and how I can please the Lord, not another man, not my earthly father, but God and God alone.

Many woman have experienced this same scenario, but the outcome may have been very different. You may have become the second woman, an adulteress, and dug yourself into a pit that you think you will never come out of. You use the man for what you can get and the time he will give you, but you are never the wife or the woman that he takes family trips with. You may be settling for your light bill being paid and the latest name brand shoes or purse, but never the woman that gets to wear the wedding ring. Or you may be a woman that has contemplated dating a married man, but you have not fully acted on the impulse. Or you may be the woman that is waiting for him to change and keep his promise that he is going to leave his wife and marry you. Please wake up! Being the second woman only leads to days, months and even years of heart-ache and disappointment. You will never be satisfied as the second woman. Stop deceiving yourself. You will only become numb and callous to the situation that you have allowed yourself to be entangled into. It's time to get out now and stay out! It will not happen overnight, but you have to start. You do deserve the best, so get out of the hurtful and damaging relationship and pursue yourself, who you were designed to be and what you were created to obtain. Start loving you, for real this time!

PRAYER

Lord, my prayer for my sister is that she will choose herself this time. She will choose who you designed her to be, a beautiful woman, and a daughter of the Most High King. I pray sister that you will have the strength to trust the Lord with all your heart, mind and soul. I pray today, that you recognize that you were born to be number one, not second best. I pray that you will know that you do not have to wait and live on broken promises, but you can have life and life more abundantly. I pray that you will fall in love with Jesus, who is your husband until the Lord brings you to the earthly husband that he has created for you. Allow the Lord to be your provider, your friend, your comforter. I pray that the Lord will heal your heart, mend you back together, and make you whole again. I pray that you find completeness in the Lord and not a man. I pray that your eyes will be open to the schemes of the devil and his temptations. Knowing that it is only a testing of your faith and trust in God. I pray that you will not grow weary in well doing, but that you will keep the faith.

EMPOWERMENT CONFESSIONS

For your husband is your Maker,
Whose name is the Lord of hosts;
And your Redeemer is the Holy One of Israel,
Who is called the God of all the earth.
Isaiah 54:5

Let us not lose heart in doing good, for in due time we will reap if
we do not grow weary.
Galatians 6:9

Trust in the Lord with all your heart
And do not lean on your own understanding.
In all your ways acknowledge Him,
And He will make your paths straight.
I pray that your eyes will be enlightened.
Proverbs 3:5-6

Therefore, my beloved brethren, be steadfast, immovable, always
abounding in the work of the Lord, knowing that your toil is not in
vain in the Lord.
I Corinthians 15:58

That the God of our Lord Jesus Christ, the Father of glory, may give
to you a spirit of wisdom and of revelation in the knowledge of Him.
I pray that the eyes of your heart may be enlightened, so that you
will know what is the hope of His calling, what are the riches of the
glory of His inheritance in the saints, and what is the surpassing
greatness of His power toward us who believe.
Ephesians 1:17-19

PART FOUR: THE PURIFICATION
WHO ARE YOU? YOUR TRUE IDENTITY

"Men, money, and material things can create your identity, if you let it. Nevertheless, you were not designed from such earthly things."
— Frenise Mann

Identity crisis is the fastest growing crime in the United States today. "Every two seconds, identity fraud hits a new victim." - CNNMoney, 2/06/2014. There were over 13.1 million victims hit by identity fraud in 2013. This statistic is a rude awakening to me when it comes to the importance of knowing who you are and who you belong too. For several years in my life, I allowed my past, men and circumstances to create and shape my identity. Trying to maintain this identity led to fear, shame, disappointment, and exhaustion. I was tired of trying to be everything to everybody, thinking this would make them happy and in turn make me happy. Wrong again. Just as identity theft is growing in the natural, so is it in the spiritual.

"The opposite of courage is not fear but conformity. Nothing in life is more exhausting and frustrating than trying to live it as someone else." – John Mason

I had to come to the realization that I did not know my true identity. Which brings us to one of the final stages of the formation of a diamond, which I call purification. Diamonds, known as the hardest precious stone, forgo extreme pressures and heat to bring them to their purest form and clarity. As the diamond is brought forth from the earth's volcanic crust, it builds layers upon layers of crystalized lattice, preparing it to be cut and shaped as the manufacturer desires. God is the manufacturer and you are the diamond. In order to come into your true identity, you must be willing to be purified by the Father.

Purification is the act or instance of cleansing, to make one free, separation or cutting away of the flesh. This process does not sound fun at all, but it is necessary for women to embrace their true identity. The world dictates who we are supposed to be through television, magazines, radio, billboards and social media 24 hours a day. The world tells us how to dress, talk, and walk through these same forms and strategies mentioned above, leading us to believe that this is happiness or success. If the world has the answer, then why are so many women depressed, lonely and confused? To become a rare jewel, one must allow God to cut away the impurities of your past circumstances. Allow Him to bring clarity and newness to your body, mind and heart. God the Father created woman and He is the only one with the true answer about our identity.

A great author once told this story:
A middle-aged woman had a heart attack and was rushed to the emergency room. On the operating table she had a near-death experience; seeing God, she asked if this was it. He said, "No, you have another forty-three years, two months, and eight days to live."

Upon recovery, she decided to stay in the hospital and have a face-lift, liposuction, a tummy tuck, the whole works. She even had someone come in and change her hair color, figuring that since she had so much life remaining, she might as well make the most of it.

She was discharged after the final procedure; however, while crossing the street outside, she was killed by a speeding ambulance.

Arriving in God's presence, she fumed, "I thought you said I had another forty-plus years. He replied, "I didn't recognize you."
— John Mason

Your true identity was not a mistake. So stop trying to be someone else, except who the Creator made you to be. Be yourself. I had to learn from my heavenly Father my true identity. How did I learn? I learned by reading and studying the word of God, praying and enjoying my season of singleness. I stopped striving for a relationship or looking for a man to complete me or tell me who I was. Only the manufacturer can tell you who He created you to be. According to the word of God, we are created in the image and likeness of God the Father, the Son and the Holy Spirit. We are created to have dominion and authority over the earth, not people. In spite of all the abuse and scars of my past, I learned that I was fearfully and wonderfully made. I recognized who God created me to be was priceless. I no longer identify myself as abused, depressed, suicidal, or a child raised by a single parent, but I receive who the Creator says that I am. As a woman of God, I was created to operate with power, authority and dominion. I was born to lead and leave a legacy upon the earth realm. I was created on purpose. In order to fully embrace my true identity, I had to allow the Father to strip off my old ways of thinking, renew my mind and forgive the people that despitefully hurt and abused me.

Many women grow up receiving their identity from their parents or the people that raised them. Or your identity is formed from the latest fashion, television sitcom, hottest video or reality show. I was no different. I wanted to please my earthly father in everything that I did. But in his absence, I began to form my identity from my relationships. As I became a young adolescent, I looked to my boyfriends to affirm and validate me. This set me on a path of false identity. From being called the girl with the big butt, to ugly and being told no one will ever want to be with you when I get through with you, my identity was shot! So all this crazy information had to be stripped off of me. Accepting Jesus Christ as my personal savior and becoming a Kingdom citizen was the beginning of my identity transformation. I no longer looked at my appearance through the eyes of the world, but through the eyes of Christ. Every detail about me from my loud laugh, curvy figure, length of my hair, and the color of my complexion was awesomely designed on purpose. I realize now that true beauty and value comes from the inside out. Anyone can change their outer appearance, but only God can make you beautiful on the inside, which flows to your outer appearance. I am now clothed in righteousness; no longer the lust, shame and guilt from my past. Strip off the elements of your past and who the world says you should identify with and embrace the woman that God created you to be.

The mind is the place that you make a decision to live or die. So many things get locked away in our minds which can be very hard to move past. We must be set free from the constant struggle of our thoughts, fears and concepts of who we think we are in our minds. You may have heard some people say, "Your mind can play tricks on you." This statement can be very true, when your mind is full of thoughts of your past, negative words from people, and ideologies of the world. As a little girl, I remember we used to say, "Sticks and stones may break your bones, but words will never hurt you." This statement is far from the truth. Words are one of the most powerful forces in the world. The mind is a battlefield, where the enemy and the world bombards us with false identities, suspicions, doubts and fears. In order to be free from these thoughts, we must renew our minds. The Bible says, "For our struggle is not against flesh and blood, but against the rulers, against the powers, against the world forces of this darkness, against the spiritual forces of wickedness in the heavenly places." - Ephesians 6:12 So in order to combat the thoughts that flood our minds on a daily basis about who we are as women, we must renew our minds with the word of God, positive confessions and prayer. The Bible says, "And do not be conformed to this world, but be transformed by the renewing of your mind, so that you may prove what the will of God is, that which is good and acceptable and perfect." - Romans 12:2 Renewing your mind takes discipline, determination and obedience. To be set free in your mind, you have to be willing to do things differently than the world dictates. Too many times we try to do things half way. We are half way living for God, and the other half is still clinging to the things of the world. I am here to tell you that this is a tactic of the enemy. The devil wants you to be lukewarm when it comes to renewing your mind. As long as you never know who you were created to be or your true identity, power and authority, the devil has defeated you. I always say, we live in a world where the world systems (television, videos, social media, reality shows) are driven into our minds about 18 hours a day. This is the subtly of the enemy to make you think that you are doing fine, when in reality you are still struggling in your mind about your true identity. You must renew your mind and focus on what the Bible says about you and not the world. You must discipline yourself not to be consumed with the world systems and set your mind on things above. "Whatever is true, whatever is honorable, whatever is right, whatever is pure, whatever is lovely, whatever is of good repute, if there is any excellence and if anything worthy of praise, dwell on these things." – Philippians 4:8

We must set our minds on things that are above and not on this earth. We will continue to struggle in our minds if we do not allow God to tear down old mindsets, cultural beliefs and strongholds. We were not created to be abused, misused, or confused. I know this now, because I choose to renew my mind every day through communication with God, the Father through prayer and His word. It is the word of God that brings about life and life more abundantly.

Furthermore, for the purification process to be complete, I had to learn to forgive. I believe that forgiveness happens continuously as you journey through life. For starters, I had to ask my heavenly Father to forgive me from all the ugly, disobedient, unkind things that I did to people before I knew the Lord. My past not only allowed me to be mistreated, but I mistreated people in my life along the way as well, due to the strongholds I was under. So the Lord sent me to several people in my past and told me to ask them for forgiveness, from my roommate in college to businesses that I worked at in high school. I then had to forgive all the people that hurt me, starting with my earthly father and mother. I mentioned earlier about my confrontation with my father and how I began the process of forgiving him. I was no longer going to allow him to repeat that untrue statement of him saying, "I did the best that I could." I truly view him as a brother in Christ and pray for him daily. When I forgave my dad, I was able to see him differently. I began to look at him through the eyes of God, not my flesh. Now, I am not going to lie to you and tell you that I do not think about all the things that I missed out on from not having a father to teach me how to receive love from the opposite sex, or being validated and affirmed in my identity. When I do think about these things, I forgive my father again, so that I can remain free in my mind. I can no longer allow the things of the past to have control over my destiny or place blame on my dad for what he did or did not do. It is a continual walk of forgiveness when it comes to my relationship with my earthly father. Sometimes I enjoy and desire his company and other times, I am not even phased by his absence. However, I intentionally stay in contact with him because there is no longer any fear, just unconditional love for him. I had to forgive my mother as well.

I have always admired my mom. When I was growing up, she was beautiful, thoughtful, strong and kind. She still carries these same qualities and characteristics today. However, when she became addicted to drugs, her demeanor changed. One of the biggest things that hurt me during the time of her addiction was that she stole money from me. During my senior year in high school, Howard, my fiancé, would send me money from his time in the military to save for our future together. Well, my mother would steal checks from the back of my checkbook, forge my signature and go and pay bills or write checks to herself and cash them. Since the checks were stolen from the back of my checkbook, it took some time for me to figure out what was happening. Of course, she denied doing it, but I knew better. Howard was furious of course, which led to more verbal and physical abuse from him. I could not understand how a mother could steal from her own child, especially since we were barely making it. I was working to support my basic needs and getting ready for college. This incident caused a major rift in our relationship, right before I headed off to college. So our relationship became estranged while I was in college. Despite, all these circumstances, I still had to forgive her to be set free and embrace my true identity. If I would have held onto who I thought I was through my upbringing, I would probably be dead today. However, when I became a believer in

Christ, I chose to forgive my parents. And I began to pray for their deliverance, my mother from drugs and my father from being a womanizer. I give God all the glory, because my prayers have been answered. My mother is no longer addicted to drugs. My relationship with both my parents have been restored and reconciled. I love them both dearly. They are very supportive of anything that I desire to do and are willing to help, if needed. I will honor them for the rest of my days on this earth, because God choose them to be my earthly parents.

The next major person I had to forgive was Howard. I would say out of all my relationships, this was the worst. I was left in despair, disappointment, and brokenness. I had to forgive myself first for allowing myself to stay in such a harsh relationship for over seven years. Once I forgave myself, then my heart was ready to forgive Howard. When I found out that he was married, I began to pray for him, his wife and children. Then the final step of forgiving Howard happened on the day that he first asked me to forgive him, at my house. The process continued as I learned to love myself, embrace my singleness and enjoy the life that God had destined for me. Even though I would call Howard the devil, he still is created in the image and likeness of God. Many times we as women in our fragile and emotional state like to blame and dwell on the past of mistreatment from the man we were with. Yet, the only person that is suffering from this dilemma is you. The man has moved on with his life, and you are still trying to figure out why you are not with someone. As long as you hold unforgiveness in your heart for the man that wreaked havoc on your life, you will continue to live in bondage. You will be stuck in the past without the capacity to move forward. Everything about us is designed to move forward, from the way our bodies are made; eyes in front of our face; to the way we were designed to walk in the natural, forward not backwards. Forgiveness is crucial to being free from your past and embracing your future. Do not allow bitterness, malice and strife to harbor in your heart. Bitterness is as sickness to your bones. You must release any person or thing that is keeping you stagnant. Disassociate yourself from people that want to continue to bring up your past. Their intentions are not good and they want to keep you in bondage. Rise up and accept your true identity. No one is holding you back, but you!

If you are struggling with your identity, then make a conscious decision to first seek God for your true identity, allow Christ to be Lord of your life, forgive the people of your past that hurt you, and renew your mind. It is not going to happen overnight. You did not get to the position you are in right now overnight, so take hold of your destiny today. Dare to be purified!

PRAYER

Lord, I pray that my sister has decided to allow you to purify her. I pray that you will allow the Father to make you over and make you new. I pray that you will begin to seek a personal relationship with the Holy Spirit. He will lead and guide you into all truth. Allow God to strip off your old mindset, your old ways of thinking. You are not your past. You are a woman of worth, value, beauty, inspiration, courage and authority. You were created to succeed and lead others. I pray the Father will reveal to you your purpose, because living on purpose is the only place where you will be fulfilled. This is your original design by the creator, for you to rule and reign. I renounce every negative word that has been spoken over your life. And I speak healing, forgiveness, virtue, love, peace, and a sound mind. I pray that you will no longer be blinded of your true identity by the cares of this world, through the world systems, television, social media, movies and talk shows. But you will sanctify yourself from these things if they do not line up with the word of God. It is God that holds the answer of why you were created. He is the manufacturer of your life! God is waiting for you to say, "Yes" to his will and His way.

EMPOWERMENT CONFESSIONS

Finally, be strong in the Lord and in the strength of His might. Put on the full armor of God, so that you will be able to stand firm against the schemes of the devil. For our struggle is not against flesh and blood, but against the rulers, against the powers, against the world forces of this darkness, against the spiritual forces of wickedness in the heavenly places.
Ephesians 6:10-12

Finally, brethren, whatever is true, whatever is honorable, whatever is right, whatever is pure, whatever is lovely, whatever is of good repute, if there is any excellence and if anything worthy of praise, dwell on these things.
Philippians 4:8
Set your mind on the things above, not on the things that are on earth.
Colossians 3:2

And do not be conformed to this world, but be transformed by the renewing of your mind, so that you may prove what the will of God is, that which is good and acceptable and perfect.
Romans 12:2

Whenever you stand praying, forgive, if you have anything against anyone, so that your Father who is in heaven will also forgive you your transgressions.
Mark 11:25

But if you do not forgive, neither will your Father who is in heaven forgive your transgressions.
Mark 11:26

So Jesus was saying to those Jews who had believed Him, "If you continue in My word, then you are truly disciples of Mine; and you will know the truth, and the truth will make you free."
John 8:31-32

Then God said, "Let Us make man in Our image, according to Our likeness; and let them have dominion over the fish of the sea and over the birds of the sky and over the cattle and over all the earth, and over every creeping thing that creeps on the earth." God created man in His own image, in the image of God He created him; male and female He created them. God blessed them; and God said to them, "Be fruitful and multiply, and fill the earth, and subdue it; and rule over the fish of the sea and over the birds of the sky and over every living thing that moves on the earth."
Genesis 1:26-28

For You formed my inward parts;
You wove me in my mother's womb.
I will give thanks to You, for I am fearfully and wonderfully made;
Wonderful are Your works, And my soul knows it very well.
Psalms 139:13-14

Honor your father and your mother, as the Lord your God has commanded you, that your days may be prolonged.
Deuteronomy 5:16

But I want you to be free from concern. One who is unmarried is concerned about the things of the Lord, how he may please the Lord.
1 Corinthians 7:32

And have put on the new self who is being renewed to a true knowledge according to the image of the One who created him.
Colossians 3:10

That if you confess with your mouth Jesus as Lord, and believe in your heart that God raised Him from the dead, you will be saved; for with the heart a person believes, resulting in righteousness, and with the mouth he confesses, resulting in salvation.
Romans 10:9-10

PART FOUR: THE PURIFICATION
WORLDLY PITFALLS AND DESIRES

This is your last chance. After this, there is no turning back. You take the blue pill - the story ends, you wake up in your bed and believe whatever you want to believe. You take the red pill - you stay in Wonderland and I show you how deep the rabbit-hole goes.
Morpheus – The Matrix Movie

Being born in a dysfunctional family and being in broken relationships are not the only struggles that women of the 21st century have to face today. As women, we hear so many remedies from our mothers/grandmothers, suggestions from talk shows, books, and magazines on how we are to live successful and fulfilled lives as a single woman that we do not really know what to believe any more. Because we have been raised without our earthly fathers, tampered with sexually against our will, abused mentally or physically through awful relationships, some women have become susceptible to believe a lie as the truth. Or you may be a women that grew up in a two-parent home, never experienced abuse, but still somehow got lost in the shuffle of life, not knowing your true identity. Whatever the case may be, if you are going to walk worthy of the calling that the Lord has bestowed upon you, then you cannot be carried away in the lust of the things of this world. The Bible tells us not to love the world nor the things in the world. "If anyone loves the world, the love of the Father is not in him." – 1 John 2:15. We as true women of God, embracing our singleness with love and satisfaction, must no longer be deceived and deluded to believe the headlines, romance novels or television shows are our reality. It may seem fun, wild and thrilling to play the role of the second woman, or live a life like the housewives, but it is just that, a role. God never intended for you to settle for what the world has to offer. So let's talk about what you have been made to believe is the truth.

I have experienced many things and heard the experiences of others. We must be willing to hold these things up against the standard, which is Jesus Christ. If it does not line up with the word of God, then it must be a lie. I want to give some insight on things that women fall for in their walk of singleness. The flesh is a "beast" and it must be resisted. Sometimes it seems as if it has its own mind, but we must have the mind of Christ. You will not win against the things of this world, unless you resist your flesh and yield to the Holy Spirit. The flesh and the Spirit are in constant struggle, therefore you cannot afford to fill your mind and thoughts with worldly advice and devices, but with the Word of God. I call these struggles worldly pitfalls and earthly desires. The things that our flesh craves to the point that we think that they are harmless or just our situation at the time. We are going to shed light upon these common pitfalls and desires. No longer will we be ensnared with these untruths. In the Matrix quote, Wonderland represents the Kingdom of God and the red pill offers salvation through Jesus Christ! So spit out the blue pill and let's go to Wonderland!

10 Worldly Pitfalls and Earthly Desires

1. "Shacking up" or living with a man will let him know that I'm ready for marriage.

According to today's Women Health magazine, nearly half of American women between the ages of 15-44 have lived with a partner before marriage. (Gueren, 2014) I'm sorry, ladies this statement is so far from the truth. Most men think compartmentally. Meaning they have thoughts that can be put in several boxes, separate from each other. This is the way a man's brain was created; although women think very differently. Most women think like a pile of spaghetti; everything is connected to everything. Women's thoughts and experiences are all connected to one another. Therefore, when it comes to "shacking up," men see this as convenience, or as having someone to have sex with regularly. They see living together as having someone to share the bills with, someone that can cook for them and possibly their children, without any obligation or commitment to share the rest of their life with you. Women see living with a man as the next step to marriage. Most women think, "If I have sex when he wants it and how he wants; if I help him get out of debt; if I just stay with him until he gets on his feet, then he will marry me." Wrong! The man you are living with is not thinking about marrying you, because he is getting all the benefits of marriage without the covenant. Some of you remember hearing the old cliché, "Why buy the cow, when the milk is free." This cliché definitely has some truth in it. A man does not care about how many times you talk about marriage or threaten to leave, as long as you keep living with him, he is not going to do anything different. Most men that you allow to live with you before marriage end up marrying someone else. And to tell the truth, the problem is not with the man, but with you, the woman. We as women must learn to love ourselves enough to wait and receive the entire kingdom. We deserve to be treated as queens, not maids. So, stop settling for being a maid and wait for the man that will not only put a ring on your finger; but will put a crown upon your head, present you before his family and friends as his queen and make you his bride. As a rare jewel, you must trust God to bring you before the man of God that he has for you, without trying the man out, like a dress you buy and try not to get deodorant on so you can take back to the store, before he marries you. You are more valuable!

2. When my man gets angry and says he is not ready for marriage, he doesn't really mean it; he is just angry. I can change his mind.

Ladies, we must stop ignoring the signs that men give us when we are dating them, thinking that he does not really mean what he is saying because soon we will be married. If a man is telling you that he is not ready for marriage, whether he is angry or not, there is probably a lot of truth to his statement. If you are living with a guy, and he still has his own place, then he is not ready for marriage. This is why every time you and your "boo" get into a heated argument, he goes to his house instead of resolving the issue. Having sex, which you may think is the answer to changing his mind, is not the answer. He is still not going to marry you, especially if you are giving him the "good-good" before marriage, whether that be some form of oral sex or vagina penetration. Many women compromise their beliefs, morals and values of their bodies, trying to change a man. If you are a believer, then your body belongs to the Lord. Too many times we wait and wait and wait, until years have gone by, and we come to recognize that our man is not going to marry us. However, you have become so emotionally involved and invested that you begin to think, "I cannot leave him now." You begin to allow your mind to be filled with questions and alternatives, such as "I do not feel like trying to get to know someone new over again," "I'm too old," "I want my children to grow up with their father in the house," " We have been together for two years; why would I leave now?" Well, my sister, we have to stop thinking so much about why we should stay in the relationship and focus on, "Why has he not married you yet?" Of course, I'm not telling you to give the man an ultimatum, that if he does not marry you then you are going to leave, because this does not work either. I am saying that you must love the Lord and yourself enough to trust and believe that God's original plan for your life was not for you to be in a relationship for years and years before a man makes you his wife. God's word says, "He has a plan for your life and it is for good and not evil, plans to give you a future that you hope for." – Jeremiah 29:11. If he is not ready to be married, then live your life as the Bible says a single woman should live, as one that pleases the Lord! Stop doing everything in your power to please this man you are with, thinking this is getting you one step closer to, "Will you marry me?" Instead, focus on pleasing the one, Jesus, who truly knows the man he has chosen to be your husband. Take all that energy and time you were spending on this man trying to change him, and put it on building a loving relationship with your Heavenly Father. I promise you, you will not be disappointed. He is the ultimate husband!!

3. Letting a man take me out for dinner or lunch doesn't cost me anything. I'm just getting a free meal.

How many times have I heard this statement, too many. Or letting a man pay a bill or two does not hurt anything; he is just helping me out. It grieves me that my sisters continue to sell themselves for a dinner at J. Alexander's or Red Lobster. We as women must believe that we deserve more than just a free meal. Let's address the idea that you may think this does not cost you anything, but it does. Number one, it costs you time invested into a relationship that is not going anywhere. It costs you emotional stress that God never intended for you to have to deal with. See, it starts off with a free meal, then we as emotional beings start thinking, "He is so nice. He would make a good husband someday." Then before you know it, you have fantasized your whole wedding, the children's names and the house you guys will live in. Once you snap back into reality, you are frustrated, because all he wanted to do was eat! When you are succumbed to this type of behavior, you are operating in manipulation, which is a form of witchcraft. Some women are so needy and starving for attention from the opposite sex that they become the user and abuser. Stop using men and allow God to provide for you. As true women of God, we must learn to be assets and not liabilities. I love the biblical story of how God brought Rebecca to her husband Isaac. Read Genesis 24. When she arrived to meet Isaac, she came on her own camels and with maid servants. If we translate that into the 21st century, she had her own stuff: lamps cars, furniture, shoes, etc. Therefore, we, as women of today, need to be able to buy and have our own possessions. We need not look for a man to pay our bills or buy our meals. Because it may seem free now, but in the end it cost you heartache.

4. I will be complete when I get married.

Growing up, most little girls played house with dolls. We played like we were mothers with children and a husband. We were bought toys, like "Barbie and Ken," dishes, Easy Bake Ovens, and doll houses. So, right out of the womb, little girls have an image in their minds to be married, keep house, and have children. Boys are raised to play outside with trucks, kill things, hunt, climb trees, and shoot a gun. Most boys never play house. Therefore getting married is usually not a burning desire for them. Men want to conquer and divide. For women, it is almost engraved upon our minds from childhood to be a wife. So the idea of marriage completing you as a women has been shaped into your mind for a long time.

I believe this thought pattern of being complete when married even goes back farther, back to Genesis. In the Bible, in Genesis chapter 3, there are a turn of events from God's original design for women. According to Genesis chapter 1:26-28, women were created in the image and likeness of God, the Father, the Son and the Holy Spirit. We were given power, dominion and authority over the fish of the sea, birds of the air, and the animals upon the earth, just as the men. We were blessed by God and told to be fruitful, multiply fill the earth and subdue it. So our original design was to operate like God and look like God with power and dominion upon the earth. We were to be productive and duplicate our image upon the earth. Being fruitful was more than just being able to have children. In Genesis chapter 2, God puts man to sleep, fashions the woman and then brings her to the man and they are joined together or married as we know it today. Everything we needed to complete us as women was given to us by God when the man was asleep. God created women for the man in marriage, but not as the person or thing to complete her. However, in Genesis chapter 3, man and woman sinned and disobeyed God. Originally, when God brought the woman to the man, the man's first words were, "this is now bone of my bone, flesh of my flesh, she shall be called woman, because she was taken out of man." After they disobeyed God, the man had a different perspective about the woman that God had created for him. In Genesis 3:21, the man now called the woman, "Eve," which meant the mother of all living. This statement from the man dramatically changed the woman's mindset of God's original design for her. The woman no longer viewed herself with power, authority and dominion, now she only viewed herself as a mother and wife. Therefore, sin has corrupted the original design for women. In order to get back to our original design, we have to acknowledge our true identity and purpose through God, not man. We must walk in our original design, realizing that we were created by God to compliment the man and to help him in marriage, not to be completed by the man.

Many women believe that marriage is the answer to all the problems in their relationship. And I believe this mindset comes from women struggling in their true identity and not knowing the original intent and purpose of why we were created. No longer shall we be deceived to think that marriage completes us. We are complete in Christ, and marriage only compliments what God has already placed in us as unique, powerful and beautiful women.

5. I don't need a man.

After being abused by my father, raped and molested by a man, and mishandled in bad relationships, I could have become very bitter against men all together. Thus making this same statement, "I don't need a man." I prayed to God that he would not allow me to be bitter towards men, so as not to miss my husband when He decided to bring him along in my life. I believe women can become bitter and have this "I don't need a man syndrome," which can lead to a feminist mindset and worse, homosexuality or lesbianism. Don't get me wrong, I am definitely for women having the same rights as men, equal pay, and the reduction of violence of men against women, but not to the extreme. I know that my original design as a women is what dictates whom I am to become in life, not the world system standards and devices. God has given women and men different roles in life, and we as women should not try to bombard our way through life to be equal with them. God has already made us equal; according to Genesis, male and female were given the power, authority, and dominion. So women, know according to the word of God that you can achieve anything with a man or without a man, and it is still called success.

When a woman allows bitterness to be stored up in her heart towards men, it can lead to perverted relationships, called lesbianism. A woman begins to hate men so much that she allows herself to be comforted by the arms of another woman, which can lead to erotic, sexually feelings. Before she knows it, she is now involved with a female and wants nothing to do with men. This is not the natural way of the Creator. I believe that God never intended for a woman to be in an intimate, sexual relationship with another women. The Bible tells us that a woman should not lie with another woman as she would lie with a man. It is not natural. Many times, women who practice homosexuality believe they were born with these desires to be with another woman. And this may be true because we are all born into sin. Therefore, a woman must choose to be born again through the blood of Jesus Christ. Women must not allow abuse, rape and violence from men to turn them into another dysfunctional relationship. You must forgive the men that have hurt you and keep your heart open to men by trusting God. If you are a woman that has experienced sexual relations with another woman, or you are in a lesbian relationship right now, there is hope. You can make a decision today to leave the relationship and seek the Lord through prayer and Bible study. You must not continue to hang around with the same people, go to the same places and do the same things that caused you to become involved in this perverse relationship. Allow God to lead you to someone for godly counsel and understanding. God can and will set you free.

6. There is nothing wrong with keeping gifts from past relationships; it was only a Valentine's card.

I used to think that this was okay as well, but I soon learned that holding on to keepsakes was causing emotional detriment in my life. Every time I would wear the rings, or carry the purses Howard bought me, it always reminded me of being with him. When I missed him, I would read old cards I kept from Valentine's Day or other special occasions. In spite of how insignificant these materials things seemed, they still kept me in bondage. They were parts of the emotional soul tie that I formed with Howard. Soul ties occur when the emotions, the mind and the will of a person becomes entangled to the point where their thoughts are no longer their own. Keeping gifts, trinkets and other material things from old relationships keeps you thinking, "What if or I wonder questions?" What if I would have done this or said that, would we still be together? I wonder what he is doing right now. What if I called him, would he answer the phone? In order to truly be set free from bad relationships, you have to get rid of all the baggage that came along with the relationship. You can take drastic measures and burn the cards, love letters, pictures, clothes, shoes and jewelry! Or you can simply throw them away. The Lord helped me get rid of my stuff. My house was broken into, and they stole the jewelry that Howard and Harrison bought me. The clothes were torn up. The shoes and purses I gave away to family. You must remove any and all things that keep you in an emotional soul tie to the past. I can understand keeping pictures if you have children together, but if not, let all things go immediately. The sooner the better.

7. B.O.B. is a girl's best friend. He keeps me from sleeping around.

The Battery Operated Boyfriend is not of God! BOB, better known as a dildo/sexual-erected toy penis, is being used by single women as a means of abstaining from sex with men. So if you are using sexual toys to give yourself sexual arousal as you would experience with a man, you are still having sex, only now with a figure of your imagination or a unfamiliar spirit. BOB is a part of the world system, created to keep women deceived. Your creator never intended for you to masturbate or use sex toys as a means not to fornicate or have sex outside of marriage. These tactics are strategies of the enemy to keep you enslaved to the world and sex. There are statistics that show that 57% of women that masturbate and use sex toys in their singleness are not satisfied sexually with their husbands upon marriage. So the very thing that you are using to keep you sexually satisfied in your singleness until you get married is the very thing that destroys your marriage when the right man finds you. The Bible says that a single person cares about pleasing the Lord, not themselves. So why have a lot of women been deluded into thinking that having sex with toys is okay? It is not. The Bible tells us in I Thessalonians 4:3-5, "It is God's will that you should be sanctified: that you should avoid sexual immorality; that each of you should learn to control your own body in a way that is holy and honorable, not in passionate lust like the pagans, who do not know God." If you profess to be a believer in Jesus Christ, then you definitely should not be participating in immoral sexual sins, such as masturbation, sex toys, or pornography. Masturbation is never ultimately satisfying because it falls short of the incredibly satisfying nature of a spiritual union with a husband. With any of God's laws, He is not trying to spoil our fun, just trying to point us to something more fulfilling, sex within the confines of marriage. (Laaser, 2014)

8. Reality television shows, like *Housewives of Atlanta*, *Married to Medicine* or *Being Mary Jane* are fun to watch. I'm only keeping up with the latest fashion and hair styles.

I find that many young women, ages 18-35 are falling for this untruth about reality shows. First and foremost, if you profess to be a believer, then watching realities shows as the ones mentioned have nothing to do with glorifying God. The shows' premises are based on drama, sex, fighting, gossip, and the lives of people that you may never get to meet. Yes, there may be a few shows that depict how a woman can own her own professional business; however, there are not enough good qualities to be able to filter out all the other garbage that a woman spends hours watching. The fashion the women portray is worldly and not modest at all. The body language that the women exude is not becoming of the Kingdom. I did some research myself, by watching a couple of episodes of *Being Mary Jane* and *Housewives of Atlanta*. It is very disappointing to think that many young and older woman feel like this is their reality. In order to be successful or feel important, many women believe they have to dress or act like these woman on the reality show. In order to dress fashionably and keep up with the latest hair styles, a woman can read and look at a magazine. So, you are only deceiving yourself when you make the statement, "that you are only watching these shows for fun." These shows are imprinting a lifestyle full of drama, sex, and violent images upon your mind and in your spirit, where woman begin to accept any and everything from the men they are dating. Or you may begin to think that it is acceptable to be in an adulteress relationship or sleep around with different men. You may think it is acceptable to be called "bitches and whores" by men or other women. The reality shows are subtly seducing you to believe the characterization the show illustrates is acceptable to be your everyday reality. FALSE! A true woman of God should not want her life to be full of drama. Your reality is more than just fashion and hair styles. Your reality should be focused on living out your purpose and destiny. The Bible tells us in I John 2:15-16, "Do not love the world nor the things of the world. If anyone loves the world, the love of the Father is not in Him. For all that is in the world, the lust of the flesh, the lust of the eye and the pride of life is not from the Father, but the world." The Bible goes on to tell us how to dress in I Timothy 2:9: "Likewise I want women to adorn themselves with proper clothing, modestly and discreetly." There is nothing discreet about the majority of fashion the women on reality shows wear. Yes, the dress is provocative, seductive and usually gets the attention of men. But the men you attract are the men that want to sleep with you, not take you home to meet their mothers. Because this type of man has already undressed you with his eyes, or better yet, the outfit that you are probably wearing does not leave much to a man's imagination of you being undressed. If you wear your clothes with your breast or cleavage exposed and your dress or pants so tight on your derriere, then a man does not have to think too hard as to what you look like undressed. This should not be! Remember when we talked about Isaac and Rebecca meeting in the Bible. The Bible also tells that "she took her veil and covered herself before she was brought before Isaac" - Genesis 24:65. Could it be that you have not met the man of God, due to the fact that you are not covered up in your apparel?

In regards to the language the women on reality shows use, it is not becoming of a woman of God. The Bible tells us in Ephesians 4:29, "Let no unwholesome word proceed from your mouth, but only such a word as is good for building someone up, according to the need." As a woman being transformed into a rare jewel, your conversation can no longer be that of a woman of the world. As a woman that desires to be different, then you must do things differently than the world. I am not telling you to dress in house coats or paper bags, but you need to make sure that you are covered discreetly.

Stop telling yourself that you are watching reality shows for fun because the emotional and mental images that you are exposing your spirit to are detrimental to your walk with the Lord. Ask yourself if the Father is pleased with what you are allowing to enter into His temple, which is your body, through your eyes. If you want your life to change? If you want to get rid of the drama in your life? Then make a decision today that you are not going to fill your days watching shows that highlight and personify the total opposite of what you would like for your life to represent and exhibit. This is a small step, but it is a step in the right direction.

9. Reading romance novels, listening to love songs or watching love movies has no effect on me.
Ladies there is nothing gray about Fifty Shades of Grey. Movies like Think Like a Man, About Last Night or Tyler Perry's Temptation are shows that can stir the sexual appetite of single women. Listening to old or new love songs can bring about so many emotions or bad experiences from the past or the present. These devices can also bring about feelings of depression and loneliness. As a single

woman, you must be very careful what you allow to enter into your eyes and ears. A lot of romance novels are considered soft pornography. Calling pornography soft does not negate that it is still porn. Reading romance novels, listening to love songs or watching movies with sex scenes in them can open your mind to other types of sexual activities, like masturbating, pornography or sex outside of marriage. If you are trying to live a life of abstinence and freedom of all things that are sexual until marriage, then participating in these types of activities could hinder your goals. Pornography is destroying families and homes with rapid force. More than 50% of porn Internet users report losing interest in sex with their partner. (Denison J. , 2014) A research study published in the latest Journal of American Medical Association: Psychiatry concludes that the more pornography a person watches, the less gray matter, connectivity and activity they have in their brain. (Denison J. , Porn Users Have Structural Brain Damage, 2014) So not only does pornography ruin intimacy with your spouse or future spouse, it is also making you stupid! Pornography is a growing addiction, faster than crack cocaine.

As a woman of God, we must turn away from the actions that are degrading our bodies and desensitizing our minds. If you want to walk in true transformation from past hurts, abuse and disappointments, then you must be willing to let the things of the world go completely. A rare jewel is pure and free from all defilements. The most costly stones, the ones that are considered priceless, are clear from imperfections or occlusions. Therefore as a woman who has been translated from darkness into light, you must walk in purity and holiness. Galatians 5:16-25 states "But I say, walk by the Spirit and you will not carry out the desires of the flesh. For the flesh sets its desire against the Spirit and the Spirit against the flesh, for these are in opposition to one another, so that you may not do the things that you please. Now the deeds of the flesh are evident, which are immorality, impurity, sensuality, idolatry, sorcery, enmities, strife, jealousy, outbursts of anger, disputes, dissensions, factions, envying, drunkenness, carousing, and things like these, of which I forewarn you just as I have forewarned you that those who practice such things shall not inherit the kingdom of God. But the fruit of the Spirit is love, joy, peace, patience, kindness, goodness, faithfulness, gentleness, self-control, against such things there is no law." Women of God walk and live by the fruit of the Spirit and do not carry out the lust of the flesh. You ask, how can one live in the spirit and not partake of the things of the world? By living a life of faith and love in God and His Word, consistently.

10. When we get married, he will no longer be verbally or physically abusive to me. Marriage changes everything.
My life is definitely an example of a woman who believed this untruth. I contribute my deception to being raised in an abusive home and being involved in abusive relationships. No one was created to be abused, verbally or physically. And marriage is not going to change the mindset of an abusive man.

Whatever characteristics the guy you are dating displays will predominantly remain the same upon marriage. For some reason women have deluded themselves to thinking that marriage is the answer for all the bad things in a relationship. Not so! Marriage only magnifies the things that you decided to ignore during the dating season. I truly believed that Howard was my savior, from the horrible ordeal that I was experiencing at home. I ignored the red flags of verbal and physical abuse he began to demonstrate in our relationship. Many women of the 21st century continue to fall prey to this worldly pitfall. The U.S. Department of Justice reports that 85 percent of domestic violence victims are women. More than two million women are assaulted by men each year in America. One in five female high school students reports being abused by a dating partner. (Denison J. , 2014)

We as women must wake up and realize we were created to be loved, and abuse is not some twisted form of love. It is not love at all. The only way a man can truly love you as you were created is by knowing love, which is God. The Bible says in I John 4:8, "The one who does not love does not know God, for God is love." I know some of you are saying, "My boyfriend does know God, but he is still showing some signs of abuse." My suggestion to you would be to go back and have a talk with your boyfriend about his conversion unto salvation. Is he truly saved? Does a he have a personal relationship with the Lord? Does he pray and read the Word of God consistently, without you initiating? Your Lord will not yoke you to a person pretending to know Him. Women must be aware of men that come to entangle them into sin. According to II Timothy 3:1-7, we should be on guard against such men as these. "But realize this, that in the last days difficult times will come. For men will be lovers of self, lovers of money, boastful, arrogant, revilers, disobedient to parents, ungrateful, unholy, unloving, irreconcilable, malicious gossips, without self-control, brutal, haters of good, treacherous, reckless, conceited, lovers of pleasure rather than lovers of God, holding to a form of godliness, although they have denied its power; Avoid such men as these. For among them are those who enter into households and captivate weak women weighed down with sins, led on by various impulses, always learning and never able to come to the knowledge of the truth."

Marriage will not change abusive behavior, only a personal relationship with God and maybe some anger management counseling. It is not the responsibility or obligation of the woman to wait until the man decides that he wants to change. You deserve more, and you were designed for more. Allow God to work on your mate as you continue to pursue the things of God in your singleness. Do not stay in an abusive relationship based on a person's promises and habitual forgiveness statements. These are tactics to keep you in bondage. Ask yourself, "Did I choose this person to be with or did God choose him for me?" Again, women stay in abusive relationships claiming that the Lord told them this person was their husband. I declare, pray and check to make sure it was the voice of

God that you heard and not some familiar spirit. God desires for your marriage to be a walking billboard example of Christ and the church. I know you are thinking, what a loaded statement that needs to be explained in greater detail, which will keep you looking for the coming of the next book.

These are only a few worldly pitfalls and desires. Many I have struggled with myself, and others I have researched and learned from other women. There are definitely more that I can mention, but I have come to recognize these ten are major strongholds in women's lives today. In order to be free, one must completely turn their life over to God. Allow him to be Lord of your life, and he will lead and guide you into all truth.

I know that it can be, so easy to get carried away with the drama of other people's lives. But don't live your life through their reality, which is scripted, cut and dramatized for your fleshly pleasure. Live your life through the word of God. The Bible will always dispel a lie and give you the truth. Now, it is your responsibility to embrace the truth. Or will you continue to live a life full of drama? Make a decision today, to get out the worldly pitfalls and deny your earthly desires, because the imprint they leave on your mind and heart are too costly.

PRAYER

Lord, I pray for my sisters eyes and mind to be enlightened with the truth. I pray that she will not be carried away with the worldly lusts and earthly desires that are portrayed by this society on a regular basis every day. Help her to realize how detrimental and damaging the love of the world can be to her inner spirit over time. I pray that she is not so easily enticed to enjoy the drama of others through television and books that it becomes her reality. Lord, I pray that my sister will set her mind on the things that are above, whatever is lovely, whatever is true, whatever is pure, let her mind dwell on these things. I pray Lord, that you will give her strength to resist the subtle of the devil devices. I pray that my sister will no longer believe a lie, but stand on the word of God as her final authority. I pray that she will allow you Jesus Christ to be Lord of her life. I pray that she will yield her thoughts, heart and body to you Lord. You are the only person that can lead her and guide her to an expected end that is full of joy and peace. Sister, I beseech you to let go of worldly desires and no longer be entangled with earthly pleasures. Seek the Lord and how you may please him and not your flesh. There is nothing impossible to them that believe. I pray, Lord, that my sister will allow you to be the voice that she yields to. Help my sister to disassociate herself away from other people that desire to live a life of drama and dysfunction. And help her to gravitate to like minds and spirits that are living sold out to you. Lord, I pray that you will be the lover of her soul.

10 Worldly Pitfalls and Earthly Desires

1. "Shacking up" or living with a man will let him know that I'm ready for marriage.

2. When my man gets angry and says he is not ready for marriage, he doesn't really mean it, he is just angry. I can change his mind.

3. Letting a man take me out for dinner or lunch doesn't cost me anything. I'm just getting a free meal.

4. I will be complete when I get married.

5. I don't need a man.

6. There is nothing wrong with keeping gifts from past relationships; it was only a Valentine's card.

7. B.O.B. is a girl's best friend. He keeps me from sleeping around.

8. Reality television shows, like *Housewives of Atlanta*, *Married to Medicine* or *Being Mary Jane* are fun to watch. I'm only keeping up with the latest fashion and hair styles.

9. Reading romance novels, listening to love songs or watching love movies has no effect on me.

10. When we get married, he will no longer be verbally or physically abusive to me. Marriage changes everything.

EMPOWERMENT CONFESSIONS TO COMBAT
WORLDLY PITFALLS AND DESIRES

Do not love the world nor the things in the world. If anyone loves the world, the love of the Father is not in him.
1 John 2:15

You [are like] unfaithful wives [having illicit love affairs with the world and breaking your marriage vow to God]! Do you not know that being the world's friend is being God's enemy? So whoever chooses to be a friend of the world takes his stand as an enemy of God.
James 4:4 Amplified

And do not be conformed to this world, but be transformed by the renewing of your mind, so that you may prove what the will of God is, that which is good and acceptable and perfect.
Romans 12:2

These are the kind of men who smooth-talk themselves into the homes of unstable and needy women and take advantage of them; women who, depressed by their sinfulness, take up with every new religious fad that calls itself "truth." They get exploited every time and never really learn the truth.
2 Timothy 3:6-9 The Message

You have already lived long enough like people who don't know God. You were immoral and followed your evil desires. You went around drinking and partying and carrying on.
1 Peter 4:3 CEV

But immorality or any impurity or greed must not even be named among you, as is proper among saints; [4] and there must be no filthiness and silly talk, or coarse jesting, which are not fitting, but rather giving of thanks.
Ephesians 5:3-4

Likewise, I want women to adorn themselves with proper clothing, modestly and discreetly, not with braided hair and gold or pearls or costly garments.
1 Timothy 2:9

Do not be deceived: "Bad company corrupts good morals."
1 Corinthians 15:33

Shun immorality and all sexual looseness [flee from impurity in thought, word, or deed]. Any other sin which a man commits is one outside the body, but he who commits sexual immorality sins against his own body.
Do you not know that your body is the temple (the very sanctuary) of the Holy Spirit Who lives within you, Whom you have received [as a Gift] from God? You are not your own,
You were bought with a price [purchased with a preciousness and paid for, made His own]. So then, honor God and bring glory to Him in your body.
1 Corinthians 6:18-20

Trust in the Lord with all your heart
And do not lean on your own understanding.
In all your ways acknowledge Him,
And He will make your paths straight.
Proverbs 3:5-6

PART FOUR: THE PURIFICATION
THE FATHER'S LOVE IS EVERLASTING

"Beautiful is the man who leaves a legacy that of shared love and life. It is he who transfers meaning, assigns significance and conveys in his loving touch the fine art and gentle shaping of a life. This man shall be called, Father." — Stella Payton

"The greatest mark of a father is how he treats his children when no one is looking." — Dan Pearce, Single Dad Laughing

"Real Fathers are Solution Providers and not a part of the problem to be solved." — Fela Durotoye

"A righteous father protects his children with his time and presence." — Howard W. Hunter

I cannot think of any need in childhood as strong as the need for a father's protection. - Sigmund Freud

To think a father's love is everlasting is an awesome compliment a daughter could give to her earthly father. However, after taking a poll to see what this statement meant to some woman today, I received startling comments, far from being complementary. Some of the comments were as follows:

- A father's love to me means support. All I ever wanted from my father was for him to support me when I was growing up.

- A father's love means nothing to me. When I was growing up my father lied so much about coming to pick me up that I began to lose respect for him. I would wait for hours on my porch just waiting for him to come and get me until my grandmother told me to come in the house because it was now dark outside and my father was not coming. As I became an adult, I wanted nothing to do with my father.

- I look at my dad as just another man because he was not there for me when I was growing up. So I treat him just like any other man. I tried to reconcile with my father; however, he has always put women before me and my siblings.

- I ask my dad to call me some time, but he told me he did not have time. When I went off to college, then he tried to come around. But I never felt as if I had my father's love.

- A father's love to me looks like whatever is left. My dad was always off building the business or with other woman. He was in the home, but never really with us. And he put other things and people before me.

- My godfather was more a dad to me than my natural father. My dad does not even know my full name nor my birthday.

- Due to family drama between my mother and father's side of the family, I never reconciled with my earthly father. My daughter would ask to go and see her grandfather; however, I kept putting it off every summer until one day I got a call that he died. My daughter was so angry with me. My daughter never got to know her grandfather or his love.

- A father's love means performance. I have to tell my dad that I love him first. If I want to see him, I have to go to him. I built my personal relationships the same way; love is based on your performance. I always feel like I have to perform to get my father's love.

I must say that if I was to be asked the same question earlier on in my life, I would have had some of the same comments: performance, broken promises, or getting the leftovers after other women in his life. But ask me now, and I will tell you that a father's love means protection, sacrifice, provider, comfort, joy, peace, and everlasting love. Because now I equate that statement with my Heavenly Father and not my earthly one.

Many women struggle with receiving or accepting their Heavenly Father's love, due to the way their earthly father treated them or continues to treat them. I believe that it is very crucial for a young lady to grow up with acceptance, validation, affirmation and the love of her earthly father. These qualities set the tone and build the foundation of a woman's relationship with the opposite sex. When a young woman feels protected, provided for and affirmed by her earthly father, then she will not look for these traits in the first man that tries to do something nice for her. She will already know how it feels to be told she is beautiful or smart. So when Mr. Slick-Rick comes on the scene giving compliments, she can say "Thank you," and move on with her day. She will not have to wonder if the compliment meant something more or not. Her emotions will be intact, and she will not be longing for affirmation from anyone, especially a man.

The absence of an earthly father in a daughter's life can leave scars of hurt, disappointment, bitterness and confusion. I know these are things that I experienced, which lead me on a path of self-destruction. I had to learn to forgive my earthly father, so that I could receive my Heavenly Father. I remember a crucial time of transformation in my life during the season that I was being healed from Howard leaving me for another woman. I will never forget this intense time of prayer I was having with the Lord. I was crying and lying prostrate on the floor, which was my normal posture with Jesus during this time of brokenness. I would be balled up in a fetal position, just remembering all the hurt, pain, and disappointment of being raised by mom and her state of addiction and my father's absence. I was thinking about the rape, the abortion and how all these things happened to me. And I heard God say, "I was there with you." He said, "The reason you survived is because I kept you from going crazy and committing suicide. My love for you is everlasting." From that day forward, I have never been the same. I came to realize that through it all my heavenly father was with me all the time. Through all the molestation, rape, abuse, promiscuity, hurt, pain and disappointment, my heavenly Father was with me. God became the lover of my soul, mind and body. Jeremiah 31:3 says, "I have loved you with an everlasting love; Therefore I have drawn you with loving kindness."

All my expectations were turned toward heaven. What did I need to do to please my heavenly Father? My relationship with my earthly father went from resentment and hatred to forgiveness and love through God's eyes. I began to look at my dad as a brother in Christ who needed deliverance and a willing heart to obey his Maker. I am able to pray for my dad, love him and honor him as the Bible instructs me. "Honor your father and mother (which is the first commandment with a promise), so that it may be well with you, and that you may live long on the earth." - Ephesians 6:2-3.

The love of God is so amazing. The Bible tells us in Romans 8:35-39, "Who shall separate us from the love of Christ? Shall tribulation, or distress, or persecution, or famine, or nakedness, or peril, or sword? As it is written, For thy sake we are killed all the day long; we are accounted as sheep for the slaughter. Nay, in all these things we are more than conquerors through him that loved us. For I am persuaded, that neither death, nor life, nor angels, nor principalities, nor powers, nor things present, nor things to come, nor height, nor depth, nor any other creature, shall be able to separate us from the love of God, which is in Christ Jesus our Lord." This scripture frees us from any mistakes or failures. It does not matter what we do or don't do, the Father loves us.

No longer shall we put ourselves in bondage to our past mistakes or circumstances beyond our control, because the Father loves us with an everlasting love. I had to accept this fact and so must you. If you are still questioning your relationship with your earthly father, forgive him and move on. You are the only person suffering and delaying your destiny. Your father is living his life. It may not be peaceful or joyful, but he lives on. Your earthly father may never apologize for missing the most important times in your life, but you still have to forgive him. Forgiveness is most beneficial to the person that extends it. A person cannot move forward with unforgiveness in their heart. It can cause sickness and depression to be stored up in your physical body. If you are in this position, then make a decision today to forgive. Set yourself free!

I have lived a fulfilled life as a single woman. I have learned my true identity, purpose and vision in life. I am able to live a successful life. I have emerged through life's dark and cruel obstacles to become a rare jewel of priceless stature. No longer does my past dictate who I am or who I will become. No longer will the enemy's worldly devises and schemes deceive me into believing a lie is the truth. I know who I am and whom I belong to. I am a daughter of a King! I am flawless to Him. I am loved and adorned. I am the apple of His eye.

No way could I have survived the journey of becoming a rare jewel without Abba Father. I had to receive the Holy Spirit and walk in His Spirit every day. God is no respecter of persons. We all have been created in His image and likeness, regardless if we know it or not. And His love for us is unconditional. "The Father's love toward us is patient, kind and is not jealous. His love does not brag and is not arrogant, does not act unbecomingly; it does not seek its own, is not provoked, does not take into account a wrong suffered. His love toward us does not rejoice in unrighteousness, but rejoices with the truth; bears all things, believes all things, hopes all things, endures all things. His love never fails." I Corinthians 13:4-8

This journey has not been easy, but amazingly rewarding. My final prayer for you is to embrace your journey of self-discovery, recognizing that you are being made into a rare jewel, which is strong, bright, purified and priceless! I pray that you received healing and deliverance. I pray for restoration and forgiveness. And most of all, I pray the love of my Heavenly Father is manifested to you, in you and through you. You are worthy, valuable and beautiful. Destined to leave an indelible mark! Believe it and receive it!

I know some of you reading this book, may be wondering if I ever meet Mr. Right? Well, I did! Stay curious my friends and look forward to the next adventures of life, MARRIAGE in my upcoming book! To be married or not to be, that is the question?

WHAT'S NEXT?

Now that you have finished the book, you may be thinking, "What do I do now?" How do I get out of the web that I am entangled in? How do I get out of this abusive relationship? How do I get my mind to stop craving worldly things?

Here are some action steps to get you started. I want you to read them and then take time to reflect and pray for God's guidance. In the Time of Reflection section below, take time to write down your own empowerment confessions to meditate on as you walk this journey of becoming a rare jewel out. I know that my heavenly Father will not disappoint. You only have to believe, have faith and trust His guidance.

ACTIONS STEPS

1. You must forgive yourself.

2. You must forgive the people that have hurt you, whether it be family, friends or boyfriends.

3. You must make a decision, to allow the Lord to be your Savior. Accept Jesus Christ as your father and king, and become a citizen of His kingdom.

4. Find a church that teaches the Bible as the final authority, believes in God and seeks His kingdom and righteousness.

5. Fall in love with the word of God, the Bible. Study and meditate on God's word. Pray and communicate with the Lord, daily.

6. Ask the Lord to lead you to godly friends with like minds and spirits. Other women that desire to live sold out to God.

7. Get off all Internet dating websites, stop watching reality shows and reading soft porn novels. Dedicate your mind, heart and body to the Lord.

The journey of becoming a rare jewel is only victorious through Jesus Christ. You cannot do it without him. He is the person that makes you priceless! For further encouragement, guidance or questions, contact me at **www.Thementorfm.com.**

TIME OF REFLECTION

_____

_____

_____

_____

_____

_____

_____

_____

TIME OF REFLECTION

Works Cited

Denison, J. (2014, June 5). *Porn Users Have Structural Brain Damage*. Retrieved from Denison Forum On Truth and Culture: http://www.denisonforum.org/cultural-commentary/1061-porn-users-have-structural-brain-damage

Denison, J. (2014, June 4). *The Price of Pornography*. Retrieved from Janet Denison: Focusing on God's Word: http://www.janetdenison.com/blog/262-the-price-of-pornography

Denison, J. (2014, May 7). *The Surprising Backlash Against Explicit Media*. Retrieved from Denison Forum On Truth And Culture: http://www.denisonforum.org/cultural-commentary/1033-the-surprising-backlash-against-explicit-media

Diamond. (n.d.). Retrieved from Wikipedia.

Gueren, C. (2014, March 12). *Should Couples Live Together Before Marriage*. Retrieved from Womens Health Magazine: http://www.womenshealthmag.com

Laaser, M. (2014). *Masturbation: The Secret That Ruins Great Sex*. Retrieved from Growthtrac- Build a Better Marriage: www.growthtrac.com/masturbation-ruins-great-sex

About the Author:

Frenise Mann, better known as "The Mentor" is a gifted speaker, life coach, and multi-faceted executive. She received her Bachelor of Science from University of Tennessee, Knoxville and her Masters of Business Administration from Virginia College. She is a certified financial counselor through Dave Ramsey Financial Peace University. She is the founder and owner of Mann Financial Coaching and Indelible Legacy. Her passion and purpose is to empower and mentor individuals to obtain financial freedom and discover their purpose, identity and vision, in order to leave an indelible mark upon the earth and a legacy for the next generation.

When Frenise is not engaged in her business endeavors, she enjoys teaching, mentoring and disciplining young women in The Word of God. She truly believes that the Word is what you live by every day. She is also a women's workshop, retreat and conference speaker.

Frenise lives in Chattanooga, TN and is happily married to Carlos Mann. She enjoys reading, watching movies, traveling and spending time with close friends and family. She believes that life should be lived without regrets, intentionally and on purpose.

You can contact Frenise Mann at:
Website: www.TheMentorFM.com
Email: TheMentorFM@gmail.com
Facebook: The Mentor FM

www.ingramcontent.com/pod-product-compliance
Lightning Source LLC
Chambersburg PA
CBHW051839090426

42736CB00011B/1875